The Book of Hollywood Quotes

Compiled by Gary Herman

Omnibus Press
London/New York/Sydney/Tokyo/Cologne

Cover design
Howard Brown
Book design
Carroll & Dempsey Limited
Picture research
Ken Carroll & Frances MacGill
Design Assistant
Peter Barwick

Acknowledgements
Photographs supplied by
Carroll & Dempsey Film Archives
The Cinema Bookshop
National Film Archives

Published by Omnibus Press
(a division of Book Sales Limited)

Exclusive distributors:
Book Sales Limited, 78 Newman Street, London W1P 3LA.
Quick Fox, 33 West 60th Street, New York, N.Y. 10023, USA.
Book Sales Pty Limited, 27 Clarendon Street, Artarmon 2064, Australia.
Music Sales GmbH, Kolner Strasse 199, D-5000 Cologne 90, West Germany.
Music Sales Corp., 4-26-22 Jingumae, Shibuya-ku, Tokyo 150, Japan.

UK ISBN 0 86001 639 0
UK Order No. OP 40542
US ISBN 0 8256 3943 3
US Order No. 030943

Typeset by DahDah Typesetters Limited, London.
Printed and bound in Great Britain by
William Clowes (Beccles) Limited
Beccles and London.

Contents

Introduction

There is something magical about the Hollywood film. It reaches out to the mass, but it touches individuals in unique and fascinating ways.

It is not hard to understand where this magic comes from. Hollywood (the place and the idea) has seen the greatest collection of talent ever assembled in one area of human endeavour. The American cinema has, in its time, offered employment to everyone from actors (naturally) to zoologists (advising on jungle films or wild-life adventures). And there have been thousands of them. This unparalleled number and variety of skills has always been dedicated to one aim – the manufacture of dreams and these dreams have become a part of everyday life across the globe. Hollywood has created an extraordinary reality full of household names and familiar faces. And one need not agree with Hollywood's version of the world to be awed by it.

It is, therefore, of quite exceptional interest to discover what the people who have lived and worked in Hollywood have to say about their lives, work, leisure and beliefs. These are the people who have invented a form of life – the Hollywood movie. Their comments are not just opinions or witticisms to be judged according to profundity or correctness. They are, in the original sense of the word, insights – rarely given opportunities to see inside the Hollywood machine. A book of quotations gathers these insights together as a paint box gathers colours. The reader will paint his or her own picture.

Of course, any book of quotations will be selective, and the resulting picture may be more impressionistic than faithfully naturalistic. For one thing, the compiler of such a book will include a high proportion of his or her own favourite quotations. This is not a bad thing – after all, it is a compiler's job to choose which of millions of words are worthy to reproduce and it is better that the compiler should use his or her own judgement than seek to appease all possible readers. A good compiler will satisfy the largest possible number of readers.

It is more regrettable that, of all the thousands of actors, directors, writers, producers and technicians whose work has built the Hollywood edifice only a few have had anything to say that is both significant and recordable. For example, there are no profundities by set-builders or make-up artists (although, in one quotation, Marlene Dietrich reflects on the make-up artists' invaluable work and, moreover, one of Hollywood's most quotable personalities, Wilson Mizner, was a hotel manager and restaurateur). This is probably because nobody has bothered to write down their thoughts and not because they haven't had any.

On the other hand, fame itself is no guarantee of quotability. There are many names here you may not recognise and many people, like Dorothy Parker or Alexander Woollcott, who are over-represented because of the standards of their contribution to Hollywood history and their public renown. However, they are included (and often included at length) because they had something to say and said it in publically accessible and usually memorable ways. If only more of Hollywood's famous names had been as witty, intelligent and opinionated as some of the city's lesser alumni, I could have filled a book ten times as long with equal enjoyment.

The Book of Hollywood Quotes is not a quiz book, a history or a technical manual. It is, on the contrary, all three – to be dipped into, studied and, wherever possible, shared with friends. Old fans of Hollywood and its foibles will find many of their favourite quotations here and a considerable number of new ones. Newcomers to Hollywood's splendour will find an introductory but nonetheless revealing guide to the 'land full of crumbling pyramids'. All readers should discover something about how movies are made and how movie people live and think. The annotated index gives a brief guide to the names and films mentioned in the text. I hope the collection will add to an appreciation of Hollywood movies, but if it only gives people as much pleasure to read as it gave me to compile, it will have succeeded well enough.

Gary Herman

OPPOSITE: HUMPHREY BOGART. FAR RIGHT: RUDOLPH VALENTINO.

Chapter 1

Pictures That Move

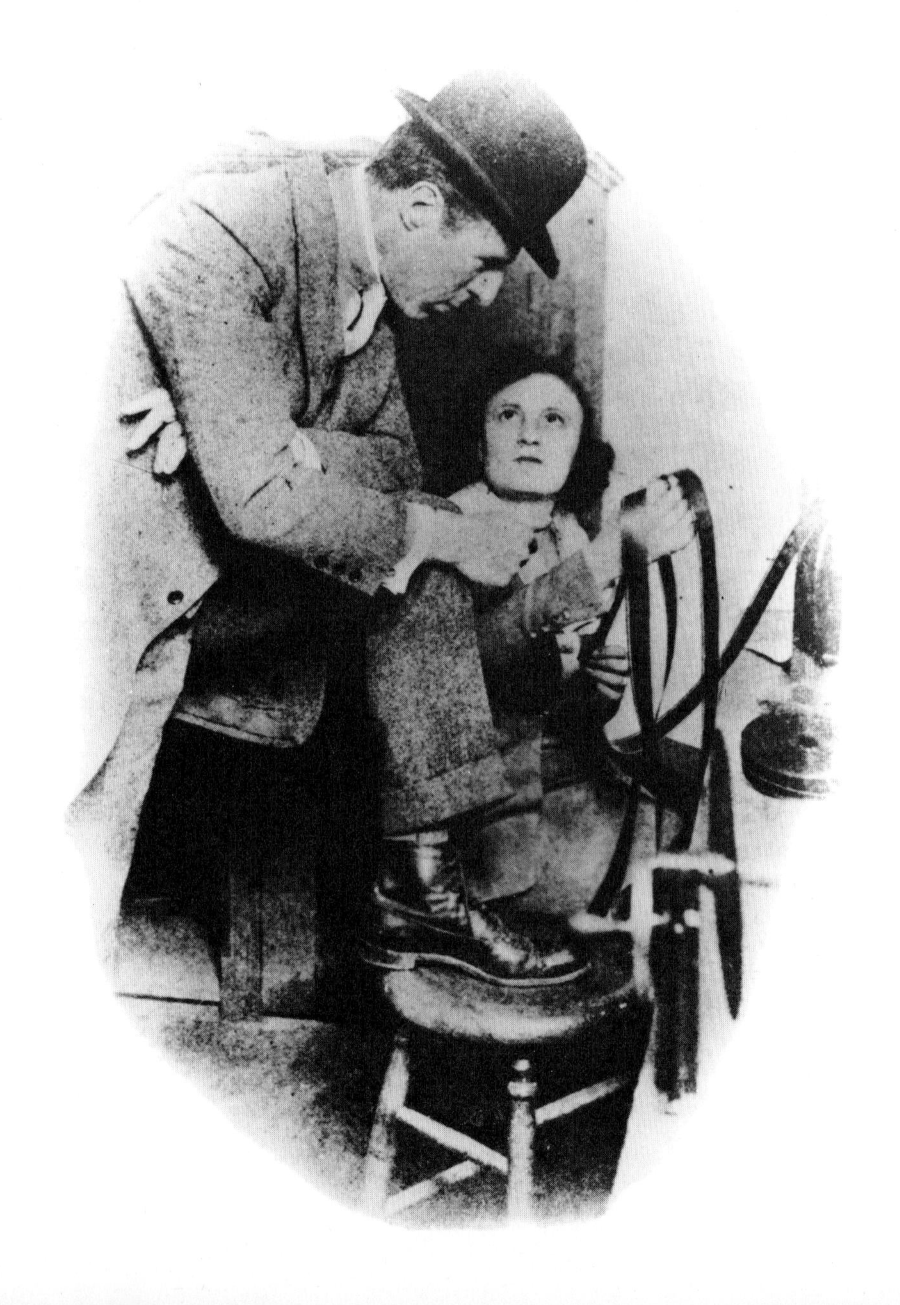

APED

BEN HECHT.

Movies were seldom written. In 1927, they were yelled into existence in conferences that kept going in saloons, brothels and all-night poker games. Movie sets roared with arguments and organ music. Sometimes little string orchestras played to help stir up the emotions of the great performers – 'Träumerei' for Clara Bow and the Meditation from 'Thaïs' for Adolphe Menjou, the screen's most sophisticated lover.
Ben Hecht.

D. W. Griffith . . . didn't have time to see pictures. He was too busy making them.
Lillian Gish.

It was a dedicated life then. You had no social life. You had to have lunch or dinner, but it was always spent talking over work – talking over stories or cutting or titles.
Lillian Gish.

Producing motion-pictures takes less brains than anything else in the world.
Lewis J. Selznick.

There is no use putting advertising where the stars won't see it. The magazines and billboards they see, with their names in big type, and it keeps them happy and contented.
Lewis J. Selznick.

A banker! A banker! I thought this business was just for furriers.
Marcus Loew,
on hearing that Joseph Kennedy had bought into the film business, 1926.

Will you accept 300 per week to work for Paramount Pictures? All expenses paid. 300 is peanuts. Millions are to be grabbed out here and your only competition is idiots. Don't let this get around.
Herman Mankiewicz,
A Telegram from him to Ben Hecht 1926.

Young man, you can be grateful that my invention is not for sale, for it would undoubtedly ruin you. It can be exploited for a certain time as a scientific curiosity, but apart from that it has no commercial value whatsoever.
Auguste Lumière,
advice on cinematography, 1895.

Making a photoplay is something like baking a cake . . . you have to have certain ingredients and know how to blend them.
Thomas Ince.

It's got to move.
Mack Sennett.

I was struck by the moral potentialities of the screen.
Adolph Zukor,
explaining his entrance into film-making.

We never make fun of religion, politics, race or mothers. A mother never gets hit with a custard-pie. Mothers-in-law, yes. But mothers, never!
Mack Sennett.

I hope I didn't make a mistake coming out here.
Carl Laemmle, 1915.

Those of us who became film producers hailed from all sorts of occupations – furriers, magicians, butchers, boilermakers – and for this reason highbrows have often poked fun at us. Yet one thing is certain – every man who succeeded was a born showman. And once in the show business he was never happy out of it.
Adolph Zukor.

I do not think that this is any monument to me, as you gentlemen have suggested, but rather a monument dedicated to America, to think that a country could give a chance to a boy like me to be connected with an institution like this.
Adolph Zukor,
at the opening of Paramount studios, 1917.

Look at that bunch of pants pressers in Hollywood making themselves millionaires. I could take the whole business away from them.
Joseph Kennedy, 1926.

Some day someone with an authentic movie mind will make a cheap and simple picture that will arrest the notice of the civilized minority . . . When that day comes, the movies will split into two halves, just as the theatre has split. There will be huge, banal, maudlin movies for the mob, and no doubt the present movie magnates will continue to produce them. And there will be movies made by artists, and for people who can read and write.
H. L. Mencken, 1927.

We had great parties at our beach house . . . during silent pictures . . . we could play cards and dance or swim. Our nights were always free, you see. It wasn't until sound came in that our entire social pattern changed. With talkies, you couldn't play at night any more – you'd come home from the studio, have supper and start studying your lines for tomorrow at eight a.m.
Bebe Daniels.

When the decision was made to change from silent films to talking films, the producers called together the greatest stars they had . . . And the producers said, 'You ladies and gentlemen who are the stars of the great silent screen, you must now learn to talk. You can no longer make faces and look camera left, camera right, up, down, what the director tells you to do, and then hope that he can put it together into a performance. You've got to learn to talk dialogue, to sustain scenes, to characterize, to remember dialogue and to play it. Those of you who can – you'll be greater than ever. Those of you who can't – overnight, no matter how great you are, you'll be finished.'
Then they called together all the great directors. And they said, 'All you directors of the silent screen, no more running out in the morning with that box, a camera and an assistant, you shoot something here, you shoot something there and then bring it back . . . You gentlemen have got to learn to read scripts, to digest characterization, pace, and how to tell a story that is written and those of you who do will be bigger than ever. Those of you who don't – overnight, you'll be forgotten.
And then they called together all the great title writers . . . and they said, 'You writers, no longer is it going to be something that you can bring in on the back of an envelope, it's no longer a question of waiting until the director gives you a film and has you write subtitles for it – you have to become dramatists – you have to learn how to write dialogue, conflict and so forth. And again, those of you who learn will go on to fabulous wealth and fame. Those of you who can't – you're finished.'
And that really happened .. . You could name the great stars of the silent screen who were finished – the great directors, gone – the great title writers who were washed up. But . . . remember this as long as you live – the producers didn't lose a man. They all made the switch. That's where the great talent is.
Ernst Lubitsch.

There never was a silent film. We'd finish a picture, show it in one of our projection rooms and come out shattered. It would be awful. We'd have

high hopes for the picture, work our heads off on it and the result was always the same. Then we'd show it in a theatre with a girl down in the pit pounding away at a piano and there would be all the difference in the world. Without that music there wouldn't have been a movie industry at all.
Irving Thalberg.

In the year 2024 the most important single thing which the cinema will have helped in a large way to accomplish will be that of eliminating from the face of the civilized world all armed conflict. Pictures will be the most powerful factor in bringing about this condition. With the use of the universal language of moving pictures the true meaning of the brotherhood of man will have been established throughout the earth. For example, the Englishman will have learned that the soul of the Japanese is, essentially, the same as his own. The Frenchman will realize that the American's ideals are his ideals. All men are created equal.
D. W. Griffith, 1924.

I was a young kid, an assistant sales manager at Universal in the East. In those days, Adolph Zukor with his Famous Players Co. was king of the business. One day Uncle Carl called me into his office. He spoke with a thick German accent. 'Yulius,' he said, 'vat's de matter ve don't get Zukor's prices for our pictures?' I was a brash, outspoken kid and I wasn't worried about losing my job, so I told him the truth. 'If we had good pictures, we'd get good prices,' I told him, 'but the truth is, Mr. Laemmle, our pictures are lousy.' Laemmle nodded his head. 'Vell, Yulius,' he said, 'if you çan't get the prices, you get the wolume.'
Jules Levy.

The lunatics have taken charge of the asylum.
Richard Rowland,
on hearing the news that Mary Pickford, Douglas Fairbanks, Charlie Chaplin and D. W. Griffith had formed their own company – United Artists.

It will never be possible to synchronize the voice with the pictures. This is true because the very nature of the films foregoes not only the necessity for but the propriety of the spoken word. Music – fine music – will always be the voice of the silent drama . . . There will never be speaking pictures.
D. W. Griffith, 1924.

Who the hell wants to hear actors talk?
H. M. Warner.

I can remember vividly how tough it was on actors and actresses when the silent pictures gave way to talkies. That microphone was a nemesis – if you didn't record well, you were finished. There was a fire one day at Paramount, and Clara Bow ran out screaming, 'I hope to Christ it was the sound stages.'
Joseph Mankiewicz.

The talkies made me sound as if I'd been castrated.
Tallulah Bankhead.

TALLULAH BANKHEAD.

Chapter 2

Hooray For Hollywood

LEFT: ORSON WELLES. RIGHT: JOHN HUSTON.

A place where great-grandmothers dread to grow old.
Phyllis Batelli.

This is Wednesday. Let me recount a little about this madhouse. In the first place Hollywood – Los Angeles – Glendale, Pasadena, etc., etc. – is one loud, struggling Main Street, low-roofed, mainly unskyscrapered town that struggles along for twenty-five miles or so, full of stop & go lights, automobiles, palm-trees, Spanishy and God knows what all houses – orange-drink stands with real orange juice – studios – movie-theatres – everything but bookstores.
Stephen Vincent Benét.

Hollywood is a place where you spend more than you make, on things you don't need, to impress people you don't like.
Ken Murray.

You can take Hollywood for granted like I did, or you can dismiss it with the contempt we reserve for what we don't understand. It can be understood too, but only dimly and in flashes.
F. Scott Fitzgerald,
'The Last Tycoon'.

It looks, it feels, as though it had been invented by a Sixth Avenue peepshow man.
Ethel Barrymore.

Hollywood is a sewer – with service from the Ritz-Carlton.
Wilson Mizner.

Hollywood is like a world's fair that's been up a year too long.
Sonny Fox.

A town that has to be seen to be disbelieved.
Walter Winchell.

Yeh, b-but you can't put k-k-ketchup on it.
Joe Frisco,
asked if he agreed that Hollywood and its environs was a beautiful place.

ETHEL BARRYMORE.

It's a great place to live – if you're an orange.
Fred Allen.

The most beautiful slave quarters in the world.
Moss Hart.

A Gentile ocean.
Oscar Levant's
description of the Pacific in the days when Californian beaches were still uninhabited.

There is the continual sunlight – the advertised palms – coolness the minute the sun sets – and plenty of people with colds. The boys go around without hats. They look like prize ears of corn. The girls, ditto.
Stephen Vincent Benét.

Poughskeepie with palms.
Anonymous.

A warm Siberia.
Anonymous.

Baghdad-by-the-sea.
Anonymous.

Hollywood is a carnival where there are no concessions.
Wilson Mizner.

Hollywood is the only town where you can wake up in the morning and listen to the birds coughing in the trees.
Joe Frisco.

Hollywood is a world with the personality of a paper cup.
Raymond Chandler.

The people are unreal. The flowers are unreal, they don't smell. The fruit is unreal, it doesn't taste of anything. The whole place is a glaring, gaudy, nightmarish set, built up in the desert.
Ethel Barrymore, 1932.

Nothing here is permanent. Once photographed, life here is ended.
David O. Selznick.

It's the biggest train set a boy ever had.
Orson Welles,
after being shown the Hollywood studio where he would make his first film.

Hollywood has always been a cage, a cage to catch our dreams.
John Huston.

This wedding of Jabberwock and the Muses called Hollywood.
Ben Hecht.

Of all the Christbitten places and business on the two hemispheres this one is the last curly kink on the pig's tail. And that's without prejudice to D. W. Griffith. I like him and think he's good. But Jesus, the movies!
Stephen Vincent Benét.

Hollywood's like Egypt. Full of crumbled pyramids. It'll never come back. It'll just keep crumbling until finally the wind blows the last studio props across the sand.
David O. Selznick, 1956.

Hollywood . . . will be a tourist spot like Tombstone, Arizona, before the century's done.
Ben Hecht, 1957.

Hollywood's all right. It's the pictures that are bad.
Orson Welles.

If you want to be a success in Hollywood, be sure and go to New York.
Bert Lahr.

A cultural boneyard.
Marlon Brando.

DOROTHY PARKER.

Oh, come my love and join with me
The oldest infant industry.
Come seek the bourne of palm and pearl,
The lovely land of boy-meets-girl.
Come grace this lotus-laden shore,
The isle of Do-What's-Done-Before.
Come curb the new and watch the old win,
Out where the streets are paved with Goldwyn.
Dorothy Parker.

Hollywood money isn't money. It's congealed snow, melts in your hand, and there you are.
Dorothy Parker, 1958.

A trip through a sewer in a glass-bottomed boat.
Wilson Mizner.

This is the only industry that finances its own blackmail.
Walter Wanger,
on Hollywood reporters.

Never in my life have I seen so many unhappy men making a hundred thousand dollars a year.
Nicholas Schenck,
after he had acquired control of MGM.

In Hollywood nothing is certain but death, and taxes and agents.
Leo Rosten.

Hollywood is bounded on the north, south, east and west by agents.
William Fadiman.

Hollywood impresses me as being ten million dollars' worth of intricate and highly ingenious machinery functioning elaborately to put skin on baloney.
George Jean Nathan.

Strip the phoney tinsel off Hollywood and you'll find the real tinsel underneath.
Oscar Levant.

Nobody ever goes to the trouble of getting anything straight about Hollywood. The ways of that town are, to the press, as dark as the practices of Tibet.
Ben Hecht,
discussing the suppression of 'Citizen Kane' by William Randolph Hearst.

Hollywood is every public man's pigeon. There is no editorial writer so dull that he can't straighten out the movies on an average of four times a year. There is no preacher who can't get at least three rousing sermons annually out of Hollywood. There is not even a Congressman so benighted that he can't speak with confidence on what ought to be done about that business out there.
Nunnally Johnson.

As long as Hollywood stands, no freeborn American need surrender to an inferiority complex. It is the greatest boon to psychiatrists since sex. Hollywood never gets the credit due to it.
Nunnally Johnson.

Nobody ever wrote about Hollywood with any seriousness until Scott Fitzgerald did 'The Last Tycoon'. Up till then, the level of Hollywood satire was all of the Kaufman-Hart school – you know, the 'Once in a Lifetime' comedy. They all had the same characters – the drunk writers, the stupid producers, the arrogant directors . . . who are all still here, too!
Nunnally Johnson.

There are a few notable exceptions, but on the whole journalism has never sired so coy a lot of Tom Thumbs.
Ben Hecht,
on Hollywood correspondents.

Our town worships success, the bitch goddess whose smile hides a taste for blood.
Hedda Hopper.

HEDDA HOPPER.

They've great respect for the dead in Hollywood, but none for the living.
Errol Flynn.

This is the only place I ever heard of where the citizens practise stabbing themselves in the back in their spare time just by way of gymnasium work-outs.
Nunnally Johnson.

For a long time, I've been worried about the problem of growing old and not having enough money for my old age. So about two years ago, I found a way to provide for my golden years, and I must say, it's given me a lot of satisfaction. I got myself a piggy bank, and every morning I slip a hundred dollar bill into it. I never miss doing this each day. It's so easy – everyone should do it. Now I find I have 76,800 dollars. And I could kick myself for not having started it earlier.
Harry Ruby.

Everybody here in Hollywood knows his business, plus music.
Alfred Newman.

The title 'little Napoleon' in Hollywood is equivalent to the title 'Mister' in any other community.
Alva Johnston.

You write stinking scripts, but you meet the people you like to be in a room with.
Charlie MacArthur,
on Hollywood's social scene.

Hollywood is a place where people from Iowa mistake each other for stars.
Fred Allen.

A town where inferior people have a way of making superior people feel inferior.
Dudley Field Malone.

Many ironic things happen in Hollywood. Overnight, idiots become geniuses and geniuses become idiots, waitresses turn into duchesses and what duchesses turn into won't bear mentioning. Overnight in Hollywood, panhandling hams blossom into Coquelins and Lorenzos and vice versa. The boulevards are crowded with royal coaches turning into pumpkins before your eyes. It's an Aladdin's Lamp of a town, and whichever way you rub it, genii jump out and make sport of the laws of gravity and sanity.
Ben Hecht.

Two of the cruelest, most primitive punishments our town deals out to those who have fallen from favour are the empty mailbox and the silent telephone.
Hedda Hopper.

WALTER PIDGEON

I was like a kept woman during my twenty-one years at MGM. Hollywood was like an expensive, beautifully run club. You didn't need to carry money. Your face was your credit card – all over the world.
Walter Pidgeon.

It's a shame to take this country away from the rattlesnakes.
D. W. Griffith.

I went out there for a thousand a week, and I worked Monday and I got fired Wednesday. The fellow who hired me was out of town Tuesday.
Nelson Algren.

Moving pictures is the cruelest business in the world. You must be like a boxer all the time, with your left hand out. I have a book printed in 1920. It is a blue list of movie greats. Only three men in that book are still working. In Europe, if an actor or director establishes himself, he lives forever. Here, if he doesn't make dough, they kick him out. Hollywood is money, money, money, and the nuts with everything else. How can any man be conceited when he sees the climb and then the awful nosedive?
Mike Curtiz.

Never buy anything you can't put on the Chief.
Anonymous.
Advice to Hollywood hopefuls who made the four-day journey from New York on the train called 'the Chief', c. 1930.

It's God's blessing to have a racetrack near one's place of employment.
John McNulty.

Everybody kisses everybody else in this crummy business all the time. It's the kissiest business in the world. You *have* to keep kissing people when you're penned up and working together the way we are. If people making a movie didn't keep kissing, they'd be at each other's throat.
Ava Gardner.

RIGHT: AVA GARDNER.

Lauren
Bacall

EDDIE CANTOR.

At (one) particular première, fans were screaming, oohing, and ahing over each luxurious limousine as it pulled up to the theatre. Suddenly there was a shocked silence, broken only by the sound of a badly missing motor in a broken-down Ford car. The crowd craned to look and listen as the driver, faultlessly dressed in evening clothes, stepped out and handed the keys to the parking attendant, who looked haughtily at the old Ford. 'What shall I do with it?' the attendant asked. 'Keep it,' said Mizner and walked blithely into the theatre.
Eddie Cantor.

What? And get hit by a meteor?
Robert Benchley,
when asked why he didn't go outside to enjoy the rays of the sun itself rather than tanning under a sunlamp.

The Garden of Allah apartments is the sort of place you'd expect to find down the rabbit hole.
Alexander Woollcott.

The place where a man can take his family and have a lovely seven-course dinner for 3,400 dollars.
George Jessel,
on Romanoff's restaurant.

Here they try to give you lunch Hollywood style – a hot dog and vintage wine.
Harry Kurnitz,
after dining at a newly opened American drugstore in Paris.

Robert Benchley,
on leaving a Hollywood restaurant and spotting a uniformed man standing by the exit:
Would you get us a taxi, please?
Uniformed Man (indignantly):
I am a rear admiral in the United States Navy!
Benchley:
All right, then. Get us a battleship.

I'll miss Hollywood. Of the twenty friends I thought I had, I'll miss the six I really had.
Lauren Bacall.

It's all right. You make a little money and get caught up on your debts. We're up to 1912 now.
Dorothy Parker,
asked how she liked working in Hollywood.

I have worked in advertising and with W. A. Brady Sr. But nowhere have I seen such shining waste, stupidity and conceit as in the business and managing end of this industry. Whoopee!
Stephen Vincent Benét.

As everybody knows who's ever lived here, all the little children in Beverly Hills are constantly being given lessons. I remember one day when George Burns' little boy came over to visit Harpo and Susan Marx's children. They were all out in the back yard, and Alex Marx started to climb up a big tree that stood out there. George's little boy stood at the bottom and when Alex came down he asked, 'Who's your climbing teacher?'
Gloria Stuart (Mrs. Arthur Sheekman).

. . . Though glamorous to the ignorant
. . This is the simplest city, a new school.
What is more nearly ours? If soul can mean the
civilization of the brain,
this is a soul,
a possible proud Florence.
Karl Shapiro, 'Hollywood'.

To survive there you need the ambition of a Latin American revolutionary, the ego of a grand opera tenor, and the physical stamina of a cow pony.
Billie Burke.

Nobody, not even people being trepanned and bastinadoed by the industry, will ever say anything derogatory to the movie business. Actors, writers, directors and producers all share in this chin-up conspiracy to keep the wonderfully fair name of Hollywood free of smirch and liver crumbs.
Ben Hecht.

Los Angeles is seventy-two suburbs in search of a city.
James Gleason,
(also attributed to Dorothy Parker).

I was sitting with Wilson Mizner in the Brown Derby one night when Rufus Le Maire, a Paramount executive, came in from having attended a première of 'Morocco'. He was all dressed up and wearing an Inverness cape. Mizner glanced up at Le Maire as he passed, turned back to me and said, 'That, my boy, sets the Jews back six hundred years.'
Joseph L. Mankiewicz.

JOSEPH L. MANKIEWICZ.

Chapter 3

Never Mind The Quality

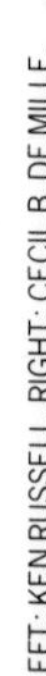

CECIL B. DE MILLE
CLEOPATRA
SPECIAL

Art is the artist's false Catholicism, the fake promise of an after-life and just as fake as heaven and hell.
Woody Allen.

I suppose the reason the studios got so powerful is that lots of directors think they don't know anything about business. I'm not sure if I know anything about business or not, but I do believe that they don't know anything about art. And if they're in business and don't know anything about art, they're not going to let art take their money.
Dennis Hopper.

The son-in-law also rises.
Anonymous
On Louis B. Mayer's appointment of his daughter's husband to an executive position at MGM.

Son-in-law of a certain studio head to songwriter Oscar Levant as Levant was playing one of his own successful songs: That's right, Oscar, play us a medley of your hit.
Oscar Levant, replying:
Okay, play us a medley of your father-in-law!

He has set the son-in-law business back twenty years.
Julius Epstein,
on an unnamed producer, married to one of the Warner brothers' daughters and responsible for a series of notable failures.

There's only one way to get into pictures if you have as little talent as I have: you have to know somebody.
Don Siegel.

CENTRE: SHIRLEY MACLAINE.

When I see the amount of money flung into that cauldron called Hollywood, I feel not one ounce of guilt about what I get. Producers have always grumbled about the money they pay us, but they keep coming back.
Shirley MacLaine.

Its trade, which is dreams at so many dollars per thousand feet, is managed by businessmen pretending to be artists and by artists pretending to be businessmen. In this queer atmosphere, nobody stays as he was; the artist begins to lose his art, and the businessman becomes temperamental and overbalanced.
J. B. Priestley, 1937.

When banks came into pictures, trouble came with them.
Cecil B. de Mille.

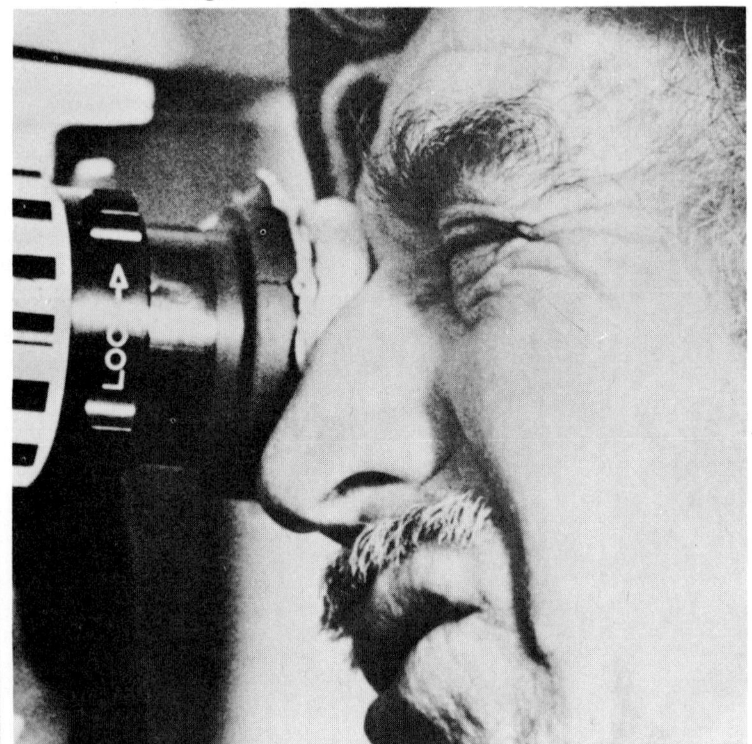

DON SIEGEL.

Jerry Mayer has a very important job and he has to have that particular office. He's supposed to watch Washington Boulevard and warn everybody to evacuate the buildings if icebergs are spotted coming down the street.
Irving Brecher,
on L. B. Mayer's brother's opulent office in the Thalberg Memorial Building.

The movies are the new literature.
Cecil B. de Mille.

When we make films in the United States, we automatically make them for the world, for the United States is full of foreigners.
Alfred Hitchcock.

I believe that although the motion picture may not live forever as a work of art, except in a few instances, it will be the most efficient way of showing posterity how we live now.
Irving Thalberg.

Film is too vast a medium for self-indulgence. It's a dangerous tool and you must be responsible when you use it.
Fritz Lang.

There are times when I wish Hollywood actors had retained the status of bums and gypsies and left the planning to others. Right now, I'm tempted to say the hell with all of it. In effect, I have complete control over everything I do. A year or two back, this was considered to be some kind of victory of Art over Tyranny. Now I'm not so sure.
Gregory Peck,
an actor who became a producer, ruminating on the fact that he had just been forced to scrap a film in mid-production.

No-one seems to want to declare his contribution to a film that bombs, whereas a hit has a hundred fathers.
Steven Spielberg.

The most important deals in the movie industry are finalised on the sun-drenched turf of golf courses or around turquoise swimming pools, where the smell of barbecue sauce is borne on gentle breezes and wafts over the stereo system of houses that people seldom leave.
Shirley MacLaine.

Carl Laemmle had all his relatives from Laupheim. Most of them were unable to do anything – you took them whether you liked them or not. Some were nice, others were arrogant bastards. The first script girl I had was a niece, and a spy for the front office. If I had caught her spying, I would have thrashed her; but oddly enough – I don't know whether it was my looks or my uniform – she didn't squeal.
Erich von Stroheim.

RIGHT: ERICH VON STROHEIM.

ERICH VON STROHEIM

The moment an audience starts to itch around you have lost them.
Fritz Lang.

Ninety-five per cent of films are born of frustration, of self-despair, of poverty, of ambition for survival, for money, for fattening bank accounts; that's what's behind 95 per cent of films. I think that 5 per cent, maybe less, are made because a man has an idea, an idea which he must express.
Samuel Fuller.

Some wag remarked bitterly, in the early days of television, that TV in two years had arrived at a mediocrity that radio had taken a quarter of a century to achieve. The same cannot be said of the movies. The ambitious struggle to achieve an audience made up exclusively of children has been long and arduous. It has been over such resisting bodies as Chaplin and Garbo and Goldwyn and Lubitsch, even Walt Disney. But the heights have been won.
Robert Ardrey.

The movie is a reflector and not an innovator.
Jack Valenti.

The cinema is not a slice of life, it's a piece of cake.
Alfred Hitchcock.

The cinema, like the detective story, makes it possible to experience without danger all the excitement, passion and desirousness which must be suppressed in a humanitarian ordering of society.
Carl Jung.

They may cost a lot, but none of the money is wasted. All my pictures can be reissued again and again. They stand up pretty well, and they retain their residual values, both financial and prestige-wise.
Sam Spiegel.

The cinema is truth twenty-four times a second.
Jean-Luc Godard.

Of all the arts, the cinema is the most important for us.
Vladimir Ilyich Lenin.

The cinema in the hands of the Soviet power represents a great and priceless force.
Joseph Stalin.

That temple of sex, with its goddesses, its guardians and its victims.
Jean Cocteau.

The film is not an art but a super tabloid for young and old, moron and genius. Her sister muses are the comic strips, the pulp magazines, the radio and all other forms of entertainment based on democratic rather than aesthetic principles.
Howard Collins.

I think there was always a political overtone in my films. With the exception of 'The Intruder', I tried not to put it on the surface, I felt it should develop out of the picture itself. If the audiences got the implications, fine; if they didn't it was just as well. I wasn't trying to push it. I feel that a film really is a two-way street, that you present something and the audience brings something and the net result is the meeting between the film and the audience, and if you say what you have to say just flatly there is no interaction.
Roger Corman.

To me, American serious movies always have one foot in entertainment – and I like more personal drama, though there may not be a market for it. The drama I like is what you see in the plays of O'Neill and Strindberg and Ibsen – and foreign films.
Woody Allen.

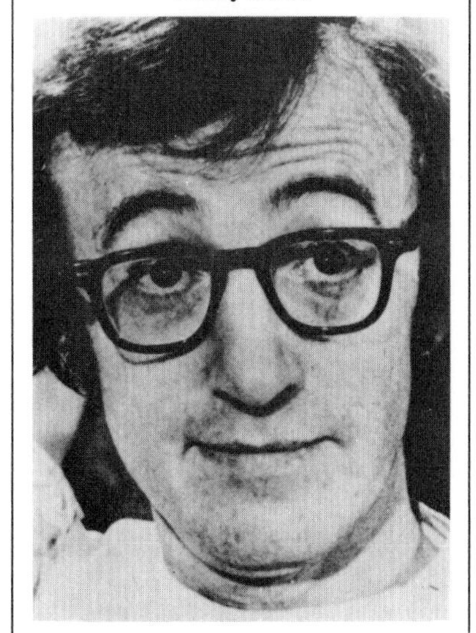

Messages are for Western Union.
Sam Goldwyn.

Drama is life with the dull bits left out.
Alfred Hitchcock.

I don't know which makes me vomit worse – the horned toads from the cloak and suit trade, the shanty Irish, or the gentlemen who talk of Screen Art.
Stephen Vincent Benét.

In 1900, Robert Fulton invented and tried to introduce the automatic or dial telephone. His invention was turned down, unwillingly, by the phone trust in compliance with a petition from people in the then infantile motion picture industry, who argued that the strain of attempting to learn the alphabet would wreak havoc with their Art.
Ring Lardner.

I try to approach film emotionally – how it moves me. I can intellectualise, but if you start out on an intellectual level, I think you're starting without the nucleus.
Clint Eastwood.

An eruption of trash that has lamed the American mind and retarded Americans from becoming cultured people.
Ben Hecht, on the movies.

There's too much pretentious nonsense talked about the artistic problems of making pictures. I've never had a goddam artistic problem in my life, never, and I've worked with the best of them.
John Wayne.

The moral is, of course, that the State should endow the cinema, as it should endow all forms of art to the extent necessary to place its highest forms above the need for competition.
George Bernard Shaw.

If all the serious lyric poets, composers, painters and sculptors were forced by law to stop their activities, a rather small fraction of the general public would become aware of the fact and a still smaller fraction would seriously regret it. If the same thing were to happen with the movies the social consequences would be catastrophic.
Erwin Panofsky.

The film is a battleground . . . love, hate, violence, action, death – in a word, *emotion*.
Sam Fuller.

Feelings of alienation, loneliness, emptiness verging on madness – those areas are all my entertainment meat.
Woody Allen.

CENTRE: WOODY ALLEN.

JOHN SCHLESINGER.

No picture can be considered a success unless it appeals to the matinee trade. When you've got a picture women want to see, the men will have to go along. But a woman can always keep a man away from a picture that only attracts him.
Irving Thalberg.

A Packard? A Cadillac? And Jack, what would my commission be – a bicycle?
Ivan Kahn, agent,
when told by Jack L. Warner that his client, Joe E. Brown, would only receive a gift of a car to appear in the Max Reinhardt film 'A Midsummer Night's Dream'.

The movies have slipped into the American mind more misinformation in one evening than the Dark Ages could muster in a decade.
Ben Hecht.

The trouble with a movie these days is that it's old before it's released. It's no accident that it comes in a can.
Orson Welles.

For me the best drama is one that deals with a man in danger.
Howard Hawks.

HOWARD HAWKS.

Making a film is like going down a mine. Once you've started you bid a metaphorical goodbye to the daylight and the outside world for the duration.
John Schlesinger.

If it's a good movie, the sound could go off and the audience would still have a perfectly clear idea of what was going on.
Alfred Hitchcock.

American movies are written by the half-educated for the half-witted.
St. John Ervine.

Movies are fun, but they're not a cure for cancer.
Warren Beatty.

Almost all serious stories in the world are stories of a failure with a death in it . . . But there is more lost paradise in them than defeat. To me that's the central theme of Western culture; the lost paradise.
Orson Welles.

Nothing is too shocking for me. When you tell the story of a man who loses his head, you have to show the head being cut off. Otherwise it's just a dirty joke without a punch line.
Roman Polanski, 1971.

This is not the age of manners. This is the age of kicking people in the crotch and telling them something and getting a reaction. I want to shock people into awareness. I don't believe there's any virtue in understatement.
Ken Russell, 1971.

The length of a film should be directly related to the endurance of the human bladder.
Alfred Hitchcock.

How long is it good?
Nicholas Schenck,
on being asked how long a film should be.

There *might* have been good movies if there had been no movie industry.
David O. Selznick.

What means this word 'pinnacle'? The public won't know what it is about. There are more blind husbands about than there are pinnacles, so we'll call it, 'Blind Husbands'.
Carl Laemmle,
to Erich von Stroheim who wanted to use the title 'The Pinnacle'.

Blessed are the deal-makers for they shall inherit the industry.
Anonymous.

I always bragged of the fact that no second of those contained in the twenty-four hours ever passed but that the name of William Fox was on the screen, being exhibited in some theatre in some part of the world.
William Fox.

If you are primarily concerned with something called personal artistic integrity, you don't belong in the business of making pictures.
David O. Selznick.

That wasn't the ending I wanted for 'Blackmail' but I had to change it for commercial reasons.
Alfred Hitchcock.

A business that can work, if it's run like a business rather than as an art form.
James Aubrey,
on the movie industry, 1971.

Boy meets girl, boy loses girl, boy gets girl.
Hollywood producers' formula, c. 1930.

Boy lays girl, boy meets girl, boy gets boy.
Producers' formula, c. 1970.

Uncle Carl Laemmle
Had a very large faemmle.
Ogden Nash.

It is as a hammer, not a mirror, that I have sought to use the medium that came to my somewhat restive hand.
John Grierson.

I don't mind coincidence – life is coincidence – but I hate convenience.
Charlie Chaplin.

A rock is a rock, a tree is a tree – shoot it in Griffith Park!
The Stern Brothers,
uncles of Carl Laemmle.

A rock is a rock, a tree is a tree, shoot it in bed.
Anonymous saying, c. **1968.**

Movies are one of the bad habits that have corrupted our century.
Ben Hecht.

When I was a freshman at Hamilton I was thrown into the college fount. In the early days of the last war, I had to take care of the bedpans in an Army hospital. But never have I been so humiliated as on my few appearances in the movies.
Alexander Woollcott.

Entertainment for the moron majority.
H. L. Mencken,
on the movies.

Who invented hokum? Think how much money he'd have made from the film producers if he'd sold his invention on a royalty basis.
Robert Sherwood.

What's history going to say about the movies? All those rows of seats facing a blank screen. Crazy!
Robert Mitchum.

You should think of each shot as you make it as the most important one in the film.
Henry Blanke.

Editing is crucial. Imagine James Stewart looking at a mother nursing a child. You see the child, then cut back to him. He smiles. Now Mr. Stewart is a benign old gentleman. Take away the middle piece of film and substitute a girl in a bikini. Now he's a dirty old man.
Alfred Hitchcock.

The cinema is the most collaborative of all the arts.
Dore Schary.

The movies are the greatest political fact in the world today.
Darryl F. Zanuck.

We are not out here to preaching with pictures, to take political sides, or bring a great message. We are here to entertain.
Mike Curtiz.

We are in this business primarily to provide entertainment, but in doing so we do not dodge the issue if we can also provide enlightenment.
Darryl F. Zanuck.

In certain pictures I do hope they will leave the cinema a little enriched, but I don't make them pay a buck and a half and then ram a lecture down their throats.
Billy Wilder.

The best motion pictures are those which reach you as entertainment, and by the time you leave have provoked thoughts. A picture that provokes no thoughts is usually not well conceived and does not entertain one anyway.
Sam Spiegel.

I don't like films with a 'message' and I think that 'entertainment' is the necessary element. You can get across a message and entertain the public at the same time and that's what is really important.
Blake Edwards.

All great American films are love stories between two men.
Anonymous.

The cinema has no boundary, it is a ribbon of dream.
Orson Welles.

JOHN FORD.

It's no use asking me to talk about art.
John Ford.

Only the first picture of a cycle really succeeds. All the imitators dwindle.
Darryl F. Zanuck.

I don't want to hold a mirror up to life as it is. I just want to show the part which is attractive – not freckled faces and broken teeth, but smooth faces and pearly white teeth.
Ross Hunter.

Reality may be very interesting, but a work of art must be a creation.
Jean Renoir.

There is no formula for success. But there is a formula for failure: and that is trying to please everybody.
Nicholas Ray.

You can fool all the people all the time if the advertising is right and the budget is big enough.
Joseph E. Levine.

Let me tell you what this business is about. It's cunt and horses!
Harry Cohn.

HARRY COHN.

Chapter 4

The Producers

A great picture has to start with a great story. Just as water can't rise higher than its source, so a picture can't rise higher than its story. The bigger the stars, the director and producer, the harder they fall on a bad story. It is the ubiquity of the 'bad story' that encumbers and impedes the screenwriter whose task is to make it into a 'good story', meaning one that will attain profitable acceptance on the screen.
Sam Goldwyn.

From quiet conferences come quiet pictures.
Sam Goldwyn.

The banks couldn't afford me. That's why I had to be in business for myself.
Sam Goldwyn,
on being an independent producer.

Sam's grasp of a script wasn't too strong when it was in screenplay form. His real genius came when the film was shot and he could see it in the projection room. There, he had an instinctive feel for what was right and wrong.
Harry Tugend.

When everybody's happy with the rushes, the picture's always a stinker.
Sam Goldwyn.

I was always an independent, even when I had partners.
Sam Goldwyn.

A producer shouldn't get ulcers, he should give them.
Sam Goldwyn.

The picture makers will inherit the earth.
Sam Goldwyn.

The big factory where movies are made is run by a super-producer called Head of the Studio who sits in the Front Office and is as difficult of access as the Grand Lama. He is the boss, appointed by the studio Owner himself. Thus, despite the veneration in which he is held by the thousand studio underlings, he is actually the greatest of the movieland stooges. He must bend his entire spirit to the philosophy of the movie Owner – 'make money.' He must translate this greedy cry of the Owner into a programme for his studio. He must examine every idea, plot or venture submitted to him from the single point of view of whether it is trite enough to appeal to the masses.
Ben Hecht.

Movie production requires producers, men who can orchestrate the sound and the fury of which pictures are made.
Joseph Kennedy.

The Hollywood producer is a man who asks a studio employee a question, gives him the answer, and then tells him why he's wrong.
Anonymous.

The job of turning good writers into movie hacks is the producer's chief task.
Ben Hecht.

A clever man whose brain starts working the moment he gets up in the morning and doesn't stop until he gets to the studio.
Martin Ragaway,
defining a producer.

Men who will keep their heads in the noisy presence of writers and directors and not be carried away by art in any of its subversive guises.
Ben Hecht, on producers.

Their task is to guard against the unusual. They are the trusted loyalists of cliché.
Ben Hecht, on producers.

What I don't see is what that producer has got to be independent about.
Tallulah Bankhead,
after seeing a bad film made by an unnamed independent producer.

Hughes never fired anybody. If he wanted to get rid of somebody, he'd merely put somebody else in over the guy.
Sam Bischoff.

The producer must be a prophet and a general, a diplomat and a peacemaker, a miser and a spendthrift. He must have vision tempered by hindsight, daring governed by caution, the patience of a saint and the iron of a Cromwell.
Jesse L. Lasky.

Boys, I've an idea. Let's fill the screen with tits.
Hunt Stromberg,
after taking over production of Robert Flaherty's 'White Shadows in the South Seas'.

I got a job at Metro . . . and I went in to see Louis Mayer, who told me he wanted me to be a producer . . . I said 'I want to write and direct,' and Mayer said, 'No! You have to produce first. You have to crawl before you walk' – which is as good a definition of producing as I've ever heard.
Joseph L. Mankiewicz.

I discovered early in my movie work that a movie is never any better than the stupidest man connected with it. There are times when this distinction may be given to the writer or director. Most often it belongs to the producer.
Ben Hecht.

Ulcers are not becoming to producers.
Jerry Wald.

There's nothing wrong with Hollywood that six first-class funerals wouldn't cure.
Anonymous, c.1930.

Sometimes you see people and you say 'that person might really be something' and you wonder where in hell they will learn . . . I think, 'if Mayer were around, that person would be a big star, maybe the first rate or the second rate.' He would develop them. (Studio heads like Mayer) cared, and they were organised, and they knew how to do it. Today, you see, they haven't got the faith in their own destiny, the people who are running the studios.
George Cukor.

I'll tell you about those men. They were monsters and pirates and bastards right down to the bottom of their feet, but they loved *movies.* They loved *making* movies, they loved *seeing* movies and they protected the people who worked for them. Some of the jerks running the business now don't even have faces.
Richard Brooks, 1970.

Fish stinks from the head.
Adolph Zukor,
head of Paramount from 1935.

The MGM lot is the Baghdad of filmdom.
Frank Capra.

I seriously object to seeing on the screen what belongs in the bedroom.
Sam Goldwyn.

Motion pictures should never embarrass a man when he brings his wife to the theatre.
Sam Goldwyn.

I make my pictures to please myself.
Sam Goldwyn.

Sam is like a Jersey cow that gives the finest milk but before you can take the bucket away he has kicked it over.
Adolph Zukor, on Sam Goldwyn.

Ken, I can't keep listening to you at this point. Let me tell you something for your own good as a writer in Hollywood. Outside of a few thousand people in Manhattan, you are the only one in the rest of America that ever reads that 'New Yorker' magazine.
Sam Goldwyn, to Ken Englund.

I'd hire the devil himself if he'd write me a good story.
Sam Goldwyn.

The trouble, Mr. Goldwyn, is that you are only interested in art – and I am only interested in money.
George Bernard Shaw,
refusing Goldwyn's offer of a job in Hollywood (also attributed to Howard Dietz, who worked for Goldwyn).

A sensitive, creative artist with a fine sense of double-entry bookkeeping.
Alexander Woollcott, on Sam Goldwyn.

I made 'Wuthering Heights'. Wyler only directed it.
Sam Goldwyn.

The trouble with this business is the dearth of bad pictures.
Sam Goldwyn.

If you can't give me your word of honour, will you give me your promise?
Sam Goldwyn.

Gentlemen – include me out!
Sam Goldwyn
(this line also appears in the Howard Hawks' film, 'Only Angels Have Wings' (1939). Goldwyn's use is unverified and undated).

Let's have some new clichés.
Sam Goldwyn.

I'll give you a definite maybe.
Sam Goldwyn.

I read part of the book right the way through.
Sam Goldwyn.

Tell me, how did you love the picture?
Sam Goldwyn,
allegedly said to a member of a preview audience.

In this business it's dog eat dog, and nobody's going to eat me.
Sam Goldwyn.

What we want is a story that starts with an earthquake and works its way up to a climax.
Sam Goldwyn.

Yes, I'm going to have a bust made of them.
Sam Goldwyn,
when his wife's hands were complimented on.

It's more than magnificent – it's mediocre.
Sam Goldwyn.

If Roosevelt were alive he'd turn in his grave.
Sam Goldwyn.

I don't care if it doesn't make a nickel. I just want every man, woman and child in America to see it.
Sam Goldwyn,
on 'The Best Years of Our Lives'.

Directors are always biting the hand that lays the golden egg.
Sam Goldwyn.

We have all passed a lot of water since then.
Sam Goldwyn.

I make fifty-two pictures a year here. Every Friday the front door opens on Gower Street and I spit a picture out. A truck picks it up and takes it away to the theatres, and that's the ball game. Now, if that door opens and I spit and nothing comes out, you and everybody else around here is out of work. So let's cut the crap about only good pictures . . . I run this place on the basis of making *one* good picture a year. I'll lay everything on the line for that one. I don't care if it's Capra, or Ford, or Riskin, or Milestone – that's the good one. The rest of them I just have to keep spitting out.
Harry Cohn,
to Robert Parrish, who had asked to be allowed to direct 'good pictures'.

Anyone who goes to a psychiatrist should have his head examined.
Sam Goldwyn.

I would be sticking my head in a moose.
Sam Goldwyn.

I had a great idea this morning, but I didn't like it.
Sam Goldwyn.

It's spreading like wildflowers.
Sam Goldwyn.

I can answer you in two words. Im Possible!
Sam Goldwyn.

Let's bring it up to date with some snappy nineteenth-century dialogue.
Sam Goldwyn.

Sam Goldwyn,
to author James Thurber, after Thurber had complained of excessive violence in the screen adaptation of 'The Secret Life Of Walter Mitty':
I am sorry you felt it was too blood and thirsty.
Thurber, replying:
Not only did I think so, but I was horror and struck.

The way I see it, my function is to be responsible for everything.
David O. Selznick.

A verbal contract isn't worth the paper it's written on.
Sam Goldwyn.

First you have a good story, then a good treatment, and next a first-rate director. After that, you hire a competent cast and even then you have only the mucus of a good picture.
Sam Goldwyn.
(Louis B. Mayer claimed that Goldwyn actually said 'nucleus' and that the malapropism was a creation of press agents).

That is the kind of ad I like. Facts. No exaggeration.
Sam Goldwyn.
On the advertisement for 'We Live Again' which read, 'The directorial skill of Mamoulian, the radiance of Anna Sten and the genius of Goldwyn have united to make the world's greatest entertainment'.

My God! The hero is a *bee*!
Sam Goldwyn,
on reading a film synopsis by Belgian symbolist writer and Nobel prizewinner, Maurice Maeterlinck, who spent the last part of his life writing about insects.

You need an automobile to reach his desk.
Sam Goldwyn, on Louis B. Mayer.

Czar of all the rushes.
B. P. Schulberg, on Louis B. Mayer.

He was, outwardly at least, a charming, simple and sincere person who could use his eyes, brimming over with tears, to convince an elephant that it was a kangaroo.
Joseph von Sternberg, on Louis B. Mayer.

An empty taxicab drove up and Louis B. Mayer got out.
Marshall Neilan.

Beautiful pictures for beautiful people.
Louis B. Mayer,
on MGM's products.

Don't show the natural functions.
Louis B. Mayer.

I only make pictures that I won't be ashamed to have my children see.
Louis B. Mayer.

A boy may hate his father but he will always respect him.
Louis B. Mayer.

Louis B. Mayer . . . is the grand Poo Bah of Hollywood. He is producing head of Metro-Goldwyn-Mayer and is not only the highest salaried genius on earth but the oracle to which Hollywood bends its ever deferential ear. It is an ear, by the way, that bends on a well-oiled hinge where Mr. Mayer is concerned.
Ben Hecht.

Who would want to laugh at a glove salesman?
Sam Goldwyn.

I want you to be sure and see my 'Hans Christian Anderson'. It's full of charmth and warmth.
Sam Goldwyn.

You should be goddamned proud kid – you should never do another thing in your life.
Sam Goldwyn,
to André Previn after hearing Previn's score for 'Porgy and Bess'.

We've got twenty-five years' worth of files out there, just sitting around. Now what I want you to do is to go out there and throw everything out – but make a copy of everything first.
Sam Goldwyn,
to one of his office clerks.

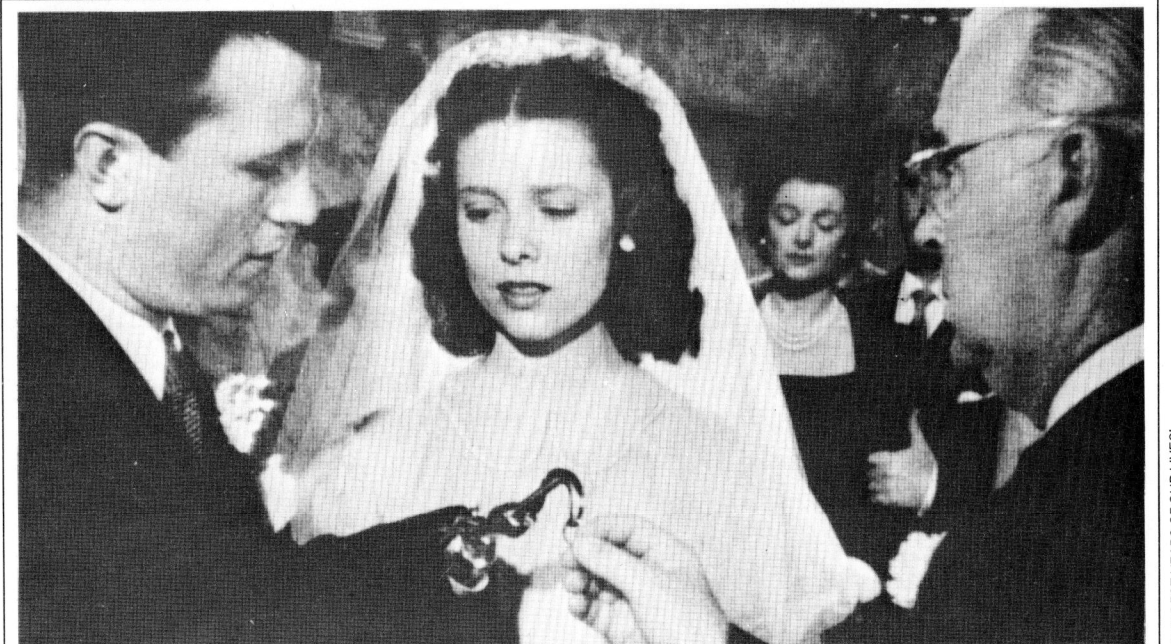

'THE BEST YEARS OF OUR LIVES'.

Tugend, this is lousy. Here I am paying you big money, and what did you do? All you did was change the words.

Sam Goldwyn
to writer Harry Tugend after Tugend had presented him with the first draft of a screen adaptation of his musical comedy 'Ball of Fire'.

It rolls off my back like a duck.
George Oppenheimer
(coined as a typical Goldwynism).

The number one book of the ages was written by a committee, and it was called the Bible.
Louis B. Mayer,
to writers who complained about their work being changed.

You know how I'm smart? I got people around me who know more than I do.
Louis B. Mayer.

Put my ashes in a box and tell the messenger to bring them to Louis B. Mayer's office with a farewell message from me. Then, when the messenger gets to Louis' desk, I want him to open the box and blow the ashes in the bastard's face.
B. P. Schulberg's
last request to his son, Budd.

I want to rule by love, not fear.
Louis B. Mayer.

I decided to become a genius. Hollywood was full of 'yes-men', so I decided to become a 'no-man'. I knocked everything, even Warner pictures. One day Jack Warner said he bet I thought I could run the studio better than he did. The following Monday morning he made me executive producer. Now that I had the job of genius, I was going to make the greatest picture of all time. I picked a man who is now one of the finest directors in the business, Mike Curtiz. I got top stars and I made 'Noah's Ark', one of the biggest flops ever turned out. Now Jack Warner and his brothers were certain I was a genius. And being a genius, I had to live that way. I took up polo, big-game hunting and skiing. It's great fun being a genius and I am going to continue playing the role.
Darryl Zanuck, 1953.

I tell you that if this scene isn't the greatest love scene ever put on film the whole goddamned picture will go right up out of the sewer.
Sam Goldwyn,
instructing Gary Cooper and Anna Sten on the set of 'Wedding Night'.

From Poland to polo in one generation.
Arthur Caesar, on Darryl Zanuck.

Take a chance and spend a million dollars and hope you're right.
Darryl F. Zanuck.

For God's sake don't say yes until I finish talking.
Darryl F. Zanuck, to an eager assistant.

There was only one boss I believed in and that was me.
Darryl F. Zanuck.

One thing we got to say about our good friend L. B. Mayer. Believe me – he's no schmuck.
George Jessel,
toasting Louis Mayer at a birthday party for the studio head (Jessel left MGM shortly afterwards).

Don't make these pictures any better. Just keep them the way they are.
Louis B. Mayer,
on the Hardy family films produced by MGM.

This is written in blank werse.
Sam Goldwyn,
on 'The Best Years of Our Lives'.

Goodbye, Mr. Zanuck. It certainly has been a pleasure working for 16th Century Fox.
Jean Renoir,
on leaving Hollywood after World War II.

I've been paying him 5,000 dollars a week for seven years and you're trying to tell me his name.
Sam Goldwyn,
after being corrected for mispronouncing Joel McCrea's name at a farewell luncheon.

You just don't realise what life is all about until you have found yourself lying on the brink of a great abscess.
Sam Goldwyn,
after recovering from a serious illness.

Why Arthur? Every Tom, Dick and Harry is called Arthur.
Sam Goldwyn,
after being told by Arthur Hornblow, Jr, that his newborn son would also be named Arthur.

You know what you did? You didn't just screw her – you screwed me!
Sam Goldwyn,
to the husband of an unnamed actress who had to give up a lead role due to an unexpected pregnancy.

David, you and I are in terrible trouble. You've got Gable and I want him.
Sam Goldwyn.
Who wanted to sign Clark Gable, to David O. Selznick, who already had him under contract.

You've got to take the bull by the teeth.
Sam Goldwyn.

The only reason so many people showed up at his funeral was because they wanted to make sure he was dead.
Sam Goldwyn,
on L. B. Mayer's funeral.

Thalberg's reticence as a movie-maker was an irritant to his fellow Pharaohs. These were gentlemen given to marching through the world with drums banging and calliopes tooting their wonders. I wrote about President Wilson in conference with our European allies at Versailles that he was like a virgin trapped in a brothel, calling sturdily for a glass of lemonade. There was about Thalberg a similar out-of-placeness.
Ben Hecht.

Louis, forget it, No Civil War picture ever made a nickel.
Irving Thalberg,
to Louis Mayer on being offered film rights to the novel 'Gone With the Wind.'

Irving knows what's right.
Louis B. Mayer.

Irving doesn't make films, he remakes them.
Anonymous comment
on Irving Thalberg's practice of editing films after preview.

It's surprising how few in this business want to make a decision. There should be more, when you consider that a man with the courage of his convictions always keeps the other fellow from knowing if *his* idea would have been a better one.
Irving Thalberg.

We should all be very happy that everyone in the world has two businesses – his own and the movies!
Irving Thalberg.

If I were a writer I would discipline myself by working on material I know very little about.
Irving Thalberg.

No story ever looks as bad as the story you've just bought; no story ever looks as good as the story the other fellow just bought.
Irving Thalberg.

On a clear day you can see Thalberg.
George S. Kaufman
on Irving Thalberg who was notorious for keeping people waiting for an audience.

I seriously began to question whether Thalberg ever existed, whether he might not be a solar myth or a deity concocted by the front office to garner prestige.
S. J. Perelman.

He's too good to last. The lamb doesn't lie down with the lion for long.
Charles MacArthur, on Irving Thalberg.

I never knew before that the entire American motion-picture audience is wired to Harry Cohn's ass.
Herman Mankiewicz,
after hearing of Harry Cohn's squirming fanny test:

Ten years of sixteen-hours-a-day work had tired him. He didn't know how to rest, or play, or even breathe without a script in his hands.
Charles MacArthur,
on Irving Thalberg's dismissal from MGM and his subsequent death.

Ah don't believe ah know which pictures are yours. Do you make the Mickey Mouse brand?
William Faulkner,
on being introduced to Irving Thalberg.

I'd drop out of sight in no time if I didn't read and keep up with current thought – and the philosophers are brain sharpeners.
Irving Thalberg,
talking about Epictetus, Kant and Bacon.

Next to D. W. Griffith, Thalberg was the greatest man in pictures . . . He had a completely fresh viewpoint on everything. He never did anything that was banal or trite. I was with him for eight years and when he died I said, 'Hollywood is finished, I'm going to get out.' And I did.
Anita Loos.

Wonders that were half mirage and half bad writing.
Ben Hecht, on MGM, 1957.

They should have kept the props and auctioned off the producers.
William Ludwig,
on the historic sale of MGM props, 1970.

If my fanny squirms, it's bad. If my fanny doesn't squirm, it's good. It's as simple as that.
Harry Cohn,
head of Columbia Pictures, claiming a totally reliable test of a picture's quality.

He was the meanest man I ever knew – an unreconstructed dinosaur.
Budd Schulberg, on Harry Cohn.

I don't have ulcers; I give them.
Harry Cohn.

Gower Street is paved with the bones of my executive producers.
Harry Cohn.

Let Rembrandt make character studies, not Columbia.
Harry Cohn.

Promise me you'll never make a picture where the characters walk out of the room backward.
Harry Cohn, to Daniel Taradash.

You had to stand in line to hate him.
Hedda Hopper, on Harry Cohn.

He liked to be the biggest bug in the manure pile.
Elia Kazan, on Harry Cohn.

All I need to make pictures is an office.
Harry Cohn.

He was a great showman and he was a son of a bitch.
George Jessel, on Harry Cohn.

He never learned how to live.
Sam Goldwyn, on Harry Cohn.

It's better than being a pimp.
Harry Cohn,
whose sexual appetite was legendary, on being a studio head.

Great parts make great pictures. Great pictures make great parts. This girl (Kim Novak) has had five hit pictures. If you want to bring me your wife or your aunt, we'll do the same for them.
Harry Cohn.

After a while the stars believe their own publicity. I've never met a grateful performer in the film business.
Harry Cohn.

We don't have temperament in our studio. We don't tolerate it.
Harry Cohn.

Harry never remembers anything unless he puts it in writing.
Anonymous studio executive, on Harry Cohn.

He's sometimes known as Harry Cohn Without Charm.
Harry Kurnitz, on Harry Cohn's brother Jack.

It proves what they always say: give the public what they want to see, and they'll come out for it.
Red Skelton,
commenting on the crowds at Harry Cohn's funeral, 1958.

If I wasn't head of a studio, who would talk to me?
Harry Cohn.

Working for Warner Brothers is like fucking a porcupine – it's one hundred pricks against one.
Wilson Mizner.

I have never gone after honours instead of dollars, but I have understood the relationship between the two.
David O. Selznick.

We should all make a killing in this business. There's so much money in the pot.
Irving Thalberg.

If you are in a position to give credit, you don't need it.
Irving Thalberg,
asked why he kept his name off the credits of his films.

For the good of the business as a whole, never let your standard be less than great.
Irving Thalberg.

Entertainment is Thalberg's god. He's content to serve him without billing, like a priest at an altar or a rabbi under the scrolls.
Charles MacArthur.

A Broadway producer with an investment of five hundred dollars in a dramatic script puts up another 500 and tells the author to work on his second act for another couple of months. I can't do that. I've got a schedule to meet. If a man brings in a script and it's got good characters and dialogue but no comedy, I get a man who can do comedy – and hope to God he won't spoil the characters. Some people are weak on character-building, and I put them to work with a man that's first-rate that way. I know they don't like it, and I don't like it myself. What can I do?
Irving Thalberg.

When I came to America twenty-five years ago to direct 'Rebecca', David Selznick sent me a memo . . . I've just finished reading it . . . I think I may turn it into a motion picture . . . I plan to call it 'The Longest Story Ever Told'.
Alfred Hitchcock, 1965.

The only Greek tragedy I know is Spyros Skouras.
Billy Wilder.
(Skouras was president of 20th-Century Fox for several years).

The great tragedy here at Fox is not so much the pictures we made but the pictures we didn't make.
Jerry Wald, 1962.

Executives can come in at nine, railroad presidents can come in at nine, bank presidents can come in at nine, why in hell can't you come in at nine?
Jack Warner,
to writers Julius and Philip Epstein, on their casual working hours.

Dear J. L. Have the bank president finish the script.
The Epsteins,
in a note to Warner attached to the first thirty pages of their next screenplay:

I can't understand it, Jack. We came in every morning at nine.
Julius Epstein,
after Jack Warner had judged a script by Julius and his brother Philip to be 'a piece of crap'.

Jack Warner has oilcloth pockets so he can steal soup.
Wilson Mizner.

John's a very headstrong, difficult man. I've tried to explain to him, we've had World War I, World War II, and now this Korean War – everywhere in America, in practically every home, there's some family with a veteran who was wounded. So I asked John, why does Gregory Peck have to have one leg?
H. M. Warner,
complaining about John Huston's expensive and ultimately unsuccessful film of 'Moby Dick' in which Peck played Ahab.

1810? When was that?
Unnamed Universal producer,
to script writer Ed Hartmann, after Hartmann had suggested that a story would work better if it was set in 1810.

The difference between me and other producers is that I am interested in the thousands and thousands of details that go into the making of a film. It is the sum total of all these things that either makes a great picture or destroys it.
David O. Selznick.

I understand that an assignment with you consists of three months work and six months recuperation.
Nunnally Johnson, to David O. Selznick.

It's somehow symbolic of Hollywood that Tara was just an empty façade with no rooms inside.
David O. Selznick,
on the house in 'Gone With the Wind'.

Very few people have mastered the art of enjoying their wealth. I have mastered the art, and therefore I spend my time enjoying myself.
David O. Selznick,
on his retirement.

Every time Paul Muni parts his beard and looks down a telescope, this company loses two million dollars.
Hal Wallis,
on Warner Brothers' excessive output of biopics in the thirties.

I have had a hand in the editing of every picture ever made by Warner Brothers.
Jack Warner.

Read it? I can't even lift it.
Jack Warner,
after Mervyn LeRoy suggested he read Harvey Allen's 'Anthony Adverse'.

I would rather take a fifty-mile hike than crawl through a book. I prefer to skip the long ones and get a synopsis from the story department.
Jack Warner.

BETTE DAVIS AND JOAN CRAWFORD WITH JACK WARNER.

Chapter 5

More Stars Than Heaven

LEFT: SPENCER TRACY. RIGHT:

Sincerely
Marion Davies

More Stars Than There Are In Heaven.
MGM promotional slogan.

An actor going into pictures has to have something special. That's what makes a star while a lot of damn good actors are passed by. The public recognises their work as good but they don't run out to see them with their three dollars for a ticket. The public goes to see the stars. I didn't invent those rules – that's just the way it is.
Clint Eastwood.

We are the only company whose assets all walk out the gates at night.
Louis B. Mayer.

Remember you are a star. Never go across the alley even to dump garbage unless you are dressed to the teeth.
Cecil B. de Mille, to Paulette Goddard.

God makes stars. It's up to the producers to find them.
Sam Goldwyn.

You make a star, you make a monster.
Sam Spiegel,
after casting Peter O'Toole in 'Lawrence of Arabia'.

You manufacture toys, you don't manufacture stars.
Joan Crawford.

Put the light where the money is.
Studio instruction to directors and cameramen.

Only the public can make a star . . . it's the studios who try to make a system out of it.
Marilyn Monroe.

MARILYN MONROE.

CENTRE: MARLON BRANDO.

Once you are a star actor, people start asking you questions about politics, astronomy, archaeology and birth-control.
Marlon Brando.

I have decided that while I am a star I will be every inch and every moment the star. Everyone from the studio gateman to the highest executive will know it.
Gloria Swanson.

Make up your mind dearheart. Do you want to be a great actor or a household word?
Laurence Olivier,
to Richard Burton during the shooting of 'Cleopatra'
– Richard Burton, replying:
Both.

Ah, that sad and bewildering moment when you are no longer the cherished darling, but must turn the corner and try to be funny.
Billie Burke.

The star system will never be eclipsed, only the names and the faces will change.
William Fadiman.

One of the main things about being successful is that I stopped being afraid of dying. I was always obsessed with death, obsessed with things ending, my career being finished. Now I'm not so much. I couldn't understand why that was for a long time, and finally I realized it's because when you're a movie star you're already dead, you're embalmed.
Dustin Hoffman.

Actors live in a cocoon of praise. They never meet the people who don't like them.
Robert Morley.

Speaking of screen stars, there's the mosquito.
Franklin Pierce Adams.

The star stands at the very centre of movie economics, and it is to his public image that all movies, no matter how high their artistic aim, are tailored.
Richard Schickel.

If you're a star you go through the front door carrying the roses, instead of through the back door carrying the garbage.
Robert Stack.

The important thing for a star is to have an interesting face. He doesn't have to move it very much. Editing and camerawork can always produce the desired illusion that a performance is being given.
George Sanders.

People who go to movies like me. I never had any promotion or big studio build-up . . . There are stars who are produced by the press – I am not one of them.
Clint Eastwood.

What the star-system represents is a typical sickness in our society – competition, competition success-oriented.
Jane Fonda.

To me being really famous is being a movie star.
Barbra Streisand.

The other day I was alone and a man came up to me and kept saying over and over again, 'You're a star, you're a star.' I thought, this year I'm a star, but what will I be next year – a black hole?
Woody Allen.

I am the unusual and do not need camera angles.
Charlie Chaplin.

I guess one of the most typical actor stories I ever heard took place at Paramount when I was there. Alan Ladd, who was then a big star, was walking down the street and one of his friends stopped him and said, 'Say, I read where your new picture starts Monday.'
'Yeah', said Ladd, 'and I haven't even read the script yet.'
'That must be kind of disturbing,' said his friend.'
'Sure is,' said Ladd. 'I don't know what I'm going to wear.'
Robert Emmett Dolan.

Everybody wants to get into the act!
Jimmy Durante.

Show me an actress who isn't a personality and I'll show you a woman who isn't a star.
Katharine Hepburn.

CHARLES LAUGHTON.

Every time I walk into a restaurant I get not only soup but an impersonation of Captain Bligh.
Charles Laughton.

Mr. Zukor, you have put the best of me in pickle for all time.
Sarah Bernhardt,
after seeing herself in Adolph Zukor's version of 'Queen Elizabeth' (1912).

You're only as good as your last picture.
Marie Dressler.

I played an unsympathetic part – myself.
Oscar Levant,
on his role in 'Humoresque'.

I allow myself to be understood as a colourful fragment in a drab world.
Errol Flynn.

I'll live this half of my life – I don't care about the other half.
Errol Flynn.

Old Errol died laughing. Can you beat that?
Telegram from Tony Britton to Trevor Howard.

The man that's out to do something has to keep in high gear all the time.
Douglas Fairbanks, Sr.

To be a success an actress must have the face of Venus, the brain of Minerva, the grace of Terpsichore, the memory of Macaulay, the figure of Juno and the hide of a rhinoceros.
Ethel Barrymore.

He's a very, very bad actor, but he absolutely loves doing it.
David Niven, on himself.

I'm a woman who's unfaithful to a million men.
Greta Garbo.

She didn't want to be famous. She wanted to be happy.
Clark Gable, on Jean Harlow.

With me it was 5 per cent talent and 95 per cent publicity.
Marion Davies.

Every man I knew had fallen in love with Gilda and wakened with me.
Rita Hayworth.
(Gilda was the character she played in her first successful film).

A girl is a girl. It's nice to be told you're successful at it.
Rita Hayworth.

When I started out I didn't have any desire to be an actress or to learn how to act. I just wanted to be famous.
Katharine Hepburn.

Brando Scalds Balls at Prince de Galles.
Marlon Brando.
A headline suggested by him after a hotel-waiter inadvertently spilt boiling water on his lap.

The monster was the best friend I ever had.
Boris Karloff.

What does 'inept' mean?
Jayne Mansfield,
on reading the reviews of her stage debut in 'Will Success Spoil Rock Hunter'.

Some people have youth, some have beauty. I have menace.
Edward G. Robinson.

Anyone who works is a fool. I don't work – I merely inflict myself on the public.
Robert Morley.

I don't pretend to be an ordinary housewife.
Elizabeth Taylor.

I want to go on until they have to shoot me.
Barbara Stanwyck.

Can't act. Can't sing. Slightly bald. Can dance a little.
Unnamed studio talent scout, on Fred Astaire.

I don't hurt the industry. The industry hurts itself, by making so many lousy movies – as if General Motors deliberately put out a bad car.
Humphrey Bogart.

I was always the guy behind the guy behind the gun.
Humphrey Bogart,
on his movie apprenticeship.

I'm a professional. I've done pretty well, don't you think? I've survived in a pretty rough business.
Humphrey Bogart.

I'm not organised. I'm tenacious.
Lily Tomlin.

I want to play the role of Jesus. I'm a logical choice. I look the part. I'm a Jew. And I'm a comedian.
Charlie Chaplin,
to a producer contemplating a 'Life of Christ', 1922.

I wouldn't act a role if it was not felt as dominating the whole story.
Orson Welles.

A lot of actors feel they've got to keep working. I do keep working. I play my own scenes. You don't have to be on a movie set to play scenes. I can throw a typewriter at somebody in my own time.
Sandra Locke.

I just put my feet in the air and move them around.
Fred Astaire.

I have no desire to prove anything by dancing. I have never used it as an outlet or as a means of expressing myself. I just dance.
Fred Astaire.

He gives her class and she gives him sex.
Katharine Hepburn, on Astaire and Rogers.

Lynn Fontanne,
reporting back to her husband, Alfred Lunt, on the results of the famous stage couple's first-ever screen test.

Alfred! It was absolutely remarkable! The camera does such wonderful things. You don't seem to have any lips, but the make-up and lighting were superb, and you looked absolutely marvellous! So handsome and striking, my darling, you have an entirely new career before you, I'm sure of it. If I were you, I'd be so delighted with what they've done. Whereas, I – well, I'm absolutely appalling! Disaster! I look like some dreadful old shrew – a hag – I simply couldn't bear to look at myself another second!

Alfred Lunt,
replying sadly:
No lips, eh?

When I cry, do you want the tears to run all the way, or should I stop them halfway down?
Margaret O'Brien, to director Henry Koster.

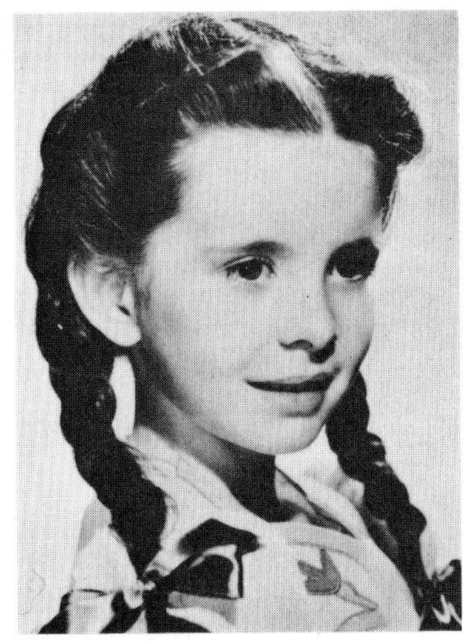

If that child had been born in the Middle Ages, she'd have been burned as a witch.
Lionel Barrymore, on Margaret O'Brien.

Put me in the last fifteen minutes of a picture and I don't care what happened before. I don't even care if I was *in* the rest of the damn thing – I'll take it in those fifteen minutes.
Barbara Stanwyck.

'Midnight' . . . was my introduction to idiot cards, flying back and forth all over the place. And boy, (John Barrymore) could start one and pick up the next like nothing. But we had this one scene where he had to walk down a narrow corridor, and with the cameras and lights and things, there was just no room for idiot cards. So I said, 'John, I'm afraid you're going to have to learn this.' He said, 'Oh? Do you want me to recite the soliloquy from "Hamlet" for you? And he did. So I said, 'Then why the hell these idiot cards?' He said, 'My dear fellow, why should I fill my mind with this shit just to forget it tomorrow morning?'
Mitchell Leisen.

My head is buried in the sands of tomorrow, while my tail feathers are singed by the hot sun of today.
John Barrymore.

If you can't make a career out of two de Milles, you'll never do it.
Charlton Heston.

There's a special excitement in playing a man who made a hole in history large enough to be remembered centuries after he died.
Charlton Heston.

The relationship between the make-up man and the film actor is that of accomplices in crime.
Marlene Dietrich.

There are two good reasons why men go to see her. Those are enough.
Howard Hughes, on Jane Russell.

Movie actors wear dark glasses to funerals to conceal the fact that their eyes are not red from weeping.
Nunnally Johnson.

I believe that God felt sorry for actors, so He created Hollywood to give them a place in the sun and a swimming pool. The price they had to pay was to surrender their talent.
Cedric Hardwicke.

They shot too many pictures and not enough actors.
Walter Winchell.

ROBERT DE NIRO.

After my first movies, I gave interviews. Then I thought, 'What's so important about where I went to school, and hobbies . . . What does any of that have to do with acting, with my own head?' Nothing.
Robert de Niro.

If you stay in front of that camera long enough, it will show you not only what you had for breakfast but who your ancestors were.
John Barrymore.

Scratch an actor and you'll find an actress.
Dorothy Parker.

No-one faintly like an actress got off the train.
Unnamed studio worker
who failed to greet Bette Davis on her arrival in Hollywood.

I was the first star who ever came out of the water looking wet.
Bette Davis.

When I saw my first film test I ran from the projection room screaming.
Bette Davis.

I came out here with one suit and everybody said I looked like a bum. Twenty years later Marlon Brando came out with only a sweat shirt and the town drools over him. That shows you how much Hollywood has progressed.
Humphrey Bogart.

Ten years ago I thought that talent equals accomplishment. You're allowed to accomplish something because you're talented, I thought. In fact, however, accomplishment equals a roll of the dice.
Sondra Locke.

I am reasonably certain that if the dramatist were alive today the movie producers would have asked Mr. Shakespeare to write in a scene in which I did physical violence to someone.
James Cagney.

Acting is the expression of a neurotic impulse.
Marlon Brando.

Acting is a bum's life. Quitting acting, that is a sign of maturity.
Marlon Brando.

His eyes mirrored the suffering we needed.
Carl Laemmle Jr., on Boris Karloff.

You could heave a brick out of the window and hit ten actors who could play my parts. I just happened to be on the right corner at the right time.
Boris Karloff.

The best way for me to prove myself as a person is to prove myself as an actress.
Marilyn Monroe.

There is as much difference between the stage and the films as between a piano and a violin. Normally you can't become a virtuoso in both.
Ethel Barrymore.

The secret of my success? I speak in a loud clear voice and try not to bump into furniture.
Alfred Lunt.

Acting is a question of absorbing other people's personalities and adding some of your own experience.
Paul Newman.

I learn the lines and pray to God.
Claude Rains.

We who play, who entertain for a few years, what can we leave that will last?
Ethel Barrymore.

I play John Wayne in every part regardless of the character, and I've been doing okay, haven't I?
John Wayne.

The idea of purposely setting out to change your image is a futile effort on the part of most actors who have become stars on the basis of what they do best.
Clint Eastwood.

In Europe an actor is an artist. In Hollywood, if he isn't working, he's a bum.
Anthony Quinn.

Acting is like roller-skating. Once you know how to do it, it is neither stimulating nor exciting.
George Sanders.

If Hollywood didn't work out I was all prepared to be the best secretary in the world.
Bette Davis.

Until I came along, all the leading men were handsome, but luckily they wrote a lot of stories about the fellow next door.
Gary Cooper.

I am paid not to think.
Clark Gable.

The King stuff is pure bull. I eat and drink and go to the bathroom just like anybody else. I'm just a lucky slob from Ohio who happened to be in the right place at the right time.
Clark Gable,
who was known as 'The King of Hollywood'.

I wasn't cut out to be an actor. I haven't the energy for acting – it's too exhausting.
Lesley Howard.

To be a successful actor . . . it is necessary to add some eccentricities and mystery to naturalness so that the audience can admire and puzzle over something different from itself.
Louise Brooks.

Halfway through the script (of 'Along Came Jones'), I ran into Coop at lunch, and I figured it would be a good idea if . . . he'd read the novel that my script was based on. 'Sure, why not?' said Coop. He was an uncomplicated fellow, one of the best guys I've ever worked with. He picked up the book and went away with it, and I went back to writing. I met him in the studio commissary a couple of weeks later. By that time I'd almost finished the first draft. 'How did you like the book, Coop?' I asked him. 'Oh, fine, I'm about halfway through,' he said. 'I'm reading it word by word.'
Nunnally Johnson.

The physical labour actors have to do wouldn't tax an embryo.
Spencer Tracy.

Only those actors appear in films who cannot sing, dance or act.
Saying, c. 1930.

I'm no actor and I never have been. What people see on the screen is me.
Clark Gable.

The best actors do not let the wheels show. This is the hardest kind of acting, and it works only if you look as if you are not acting at all.
Henry Fonda.

CENTRE: CLAUDE RAINS.

HENRY FONDA.

My talent falls within definite limits. I'm not a versatile actress.
Greta Garbo.

I don't go around shooting off my mouth about the problems of acting. In fact I don't even call myself an actor. I'm a re-actor.
John Wayne.

Once I get ahold of a character, get ahold of their essence, I'm just as excited the next time I create it.
Lily Tomlin.

I really believe in the work effort. I like people who work on things.
Diane Keaton.

An actor's a guy who, if you ain't talking about him, ain't listening.
Marlon Brando.

Death scenes are dearer than life to the actor.
Louise Brooks.

I was fortunate to be born with a set of characteristics that were in the public vogue.
Katharine Hepburn.

What's left of her.
Tallulah Bankhead,
when asked towards the end of her life if she was the famous Tallulah?

The minute you feel you have given a faultless performance is the time to get out.
Charlton Heston.

Can you imagine being wonderfully overpaid for dressing up and playing games?
David Niven.

DAVID NIVEN.

LAURENCE OLIVIER.

Would people applaud me if I were a good plumber?
Marlon Brando.

Why do actors think they're so goddam important? They're not. Acting is not an important job in the scheme of things. Plumbing is.
Spencer Tracy.

There's nothing so offensive to me as watching an actor with his ego. Some of the old movie stars were terrific but they romanticised. People chase illusions and these illusions are created by the movies. I want to make things concrete and real and to break down the illusion. There's nothing more ironic or strange or contradictory than life itself. What I try to do is make things as clear and as authentic as possible.
Robert de Niro.

Invested with great words or with the majesty of a noble thought, the actor is often confused with the source of power; once deprived of that which makes him seem magnificent he deflated like an empty windbag.
Joseph von Sternberg.

Acting is a masochistic form of exhibitionism. It is not quite the occupation of an adult.
Laurence Olivier.

I think Spencer always thought that acting was a rather silly way for a man to make a living.
Katharine Hepburn, on Spencer Tracy.

The guy's good. There's nobody in the business who can touch him and you're a fool to try. And the bastard knows it so don't fall for that humble stuff.
Clark Gable, on Spencer Tracy.

One should never praise a good actor; but always blame a bad one.
Peter Brooke.

I'm a Utopian anarchist – which means nothing. You know, the intellectuals take over and the government crumbles. I'm a less than convincing dilettante, much less an intellectual. I go to the store for a loaf of bread and come back with a quart of milk. So I act. To compensate for this indignity they put roses in the dressing room on the first day of shooting.
Robert Mitchum.

I think that being an actor . . . you lay yourself on the line . . . I'm very involved in expressing myself; hopefully, I'm not a fool for doing it; hopefully, there's some merit in it – even if it's just amusing, that's okay. It's a balance, you see, you have to watch it. I don't think you ever work out that conflict.
Diane Keaton.

I don't suppose I've seen a film of mine in years now. Frankly, I find the idea of staring at oneself on the screen decidedly unappealing.
Jack Palance.

After 'The Wizard of Oz' I was typecast as a lion, and there aren't all that many parts for lions.
Bert Lahr.

I got all the schooling any actress needs. That is, I learned to write enough to sign contracts.
Hermione Gingold.

Whatever success I've had is a lot of instinct and a little luck. I just go by how I feel.
Clint Eastwood.

The main thing in acting is not to show, not to indicate, because people don't indicate. Like, I know I run into people who had tragic things happen in their life. Their wife was raped and murdered and so on. And they tell me the story, they tell it flat, no drama, no retching, no nothing. You see the scene on television and right away the tears start coming. And that's not the way it is.
Robert de Niro.

A lot of actors don't condition themselves to long periods of hard physical effort. Towards the end of the day it shows in their performances.
Clint Eastwood.

The actor who thinks too much is troubled by one ambition: to be great. This is a terrible obstacle and it carries with it the risk that his playing may be deprived of much of its truthfulness.
Michaelangelo Antonioni.

They used to photograph Shirley Temple through gauze. They should photograph me through linoleum.
Tallulah Bankhead.

People think actresses find public-speaking easy, and it's not easy at all; we're used to hiding behind masks.
Jane Fonda.

To just do nothing but sing like a good jazz singer is *hard.*
Liza Minnelli.

His acting is largely confined to protruding his large, almost occult eyes until the vast areas of white are visible, drawing back the lips of his wide, sensuous mouth to bare his gleaming teeth, and flaring his nostrils.
Adolph Zukor, on Rudolph Valentino.

The biggest disappointment about working in films is that once you realise it's all ridiculous, there's not that much to feel strongly about. When you understand how little is possible here, there's nothing to get excited about.
Sondra Locke.

It sure beats working.
Robert Mitchum, on acting.

Everyone imitated my fuller mouth, darker eyebrows. But I wouldn't copy anybody. If I can't be me, I don't want to be anybody. I was born that way.
Joan Crawford.

Once Bogart grasped the idea that he too might achieve success with some version of natural acting, he went about its contrivance with the cunning of a lover. For all actors know that truly natural acting is rejected by the audience.
Louise Brooks.

Spence is the best we have, because you don't see the mechanism working.
Humphrey Bogart, on Spencer Tracy.

Do I subscribe to the Olivier school of acting? Ah nuts! I'm an actor. I just do what comes naturally.
Humphrey Bogart.

HUMPHREY BOGART IN 'CASABLANCA'.

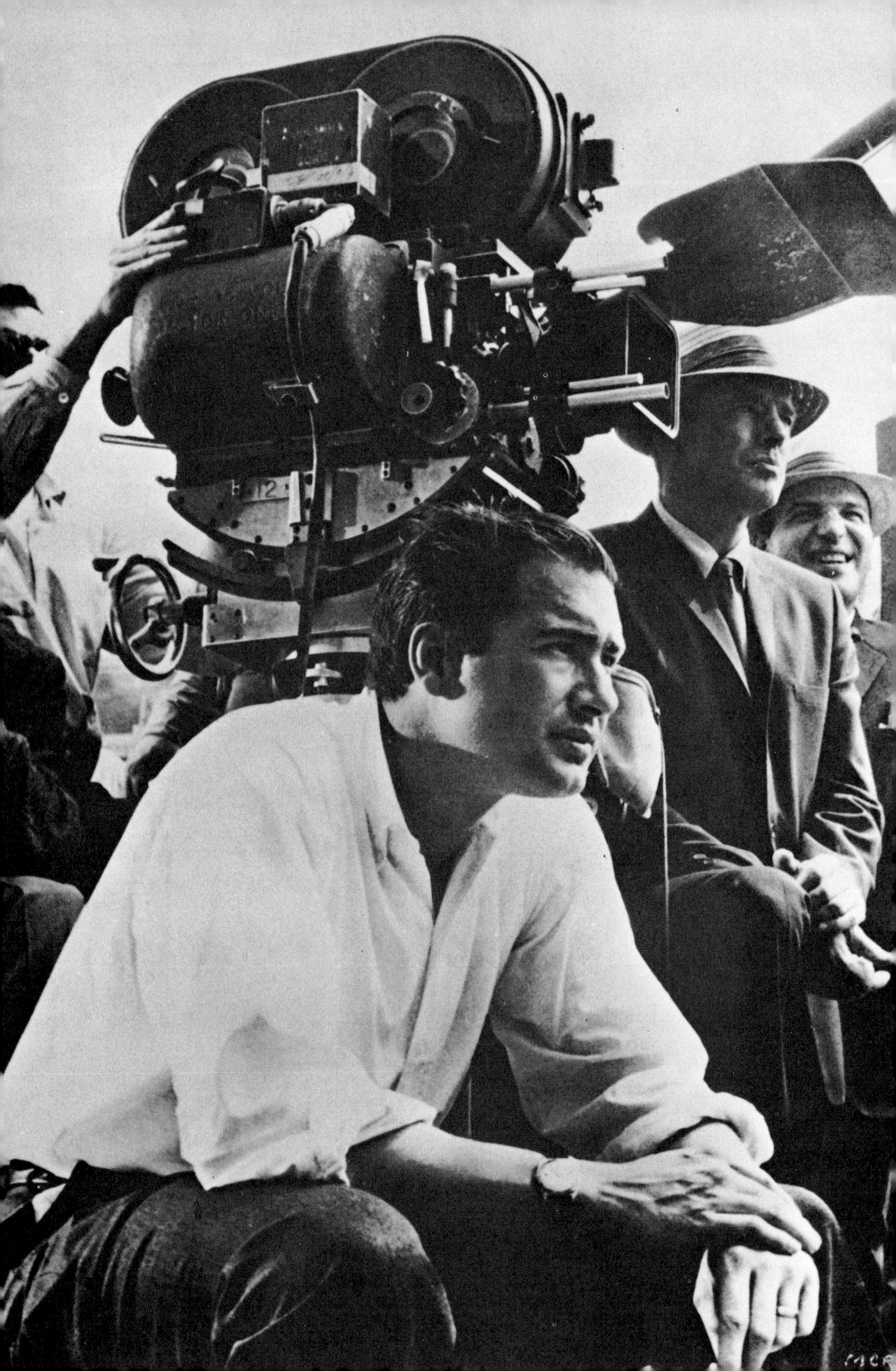

Chapter 6

Acting Under Orders

LEFT: JOHN FRANKENHEIMER ON LOCATION FOR 'YOUNG SAVAGES'. RIGHT: NORMAN JEWISON.

Don't act – think!
F. W. Murnau.

Film acting is unquestionably a director's medium.
Charlie Chaplin.

He inspired in us a belief that we were working a medium that was powerful enough to influence the whole world.
Lillian Gish, on D. W. Griffith.

Lubitsch's method of direction was perfect for me. He would act out the whole scene – and then he'd say, 'Now let's see how you'd do it.'
Jack Benny.

Actors are cattle.
Alfred Hitchcock.
(Hitchcock claims this is a misquotation of 'Actors should be treated like cattle'.)

Hitchcock said actors are cattle, but show me a cow who can earn a million dollars a film.
Michael Winner.

She was like a horse on the track. Nothing, and then the bell goes, and something happens.
James Wong Howe, on Greta Garbo.

With him acting was an act of childbirth. What he needed was not so much a director as a midwife.
Alexander Korda, on Charles Laughton.

You can't direct a Laughton picture. The best you can hope for is to referee.
Alfred Hitchcock.

There's always been one boss on a picture, the director. I haven't always agreed with him, but I've paid attention.
John Wayne.

Always cast against the part and it won't be boring.
David Lean.

DAVID LEAN.

CAROLE LOMBARD.

I can't win working with Welles. If the picture's a hit he will get the credit. If it's a flop I'll be blamed.
Carole Lombard, refusing a role.

John Ford isn't exactly a bum, is he? Yet he never gave me any manure about art. He just made movies and that's what I do.
John Wayne.

That's how to make'em good actors. Don't let any of 'em talk!
John Ford,
pointing out to Robert Parrish the source of his peculiar success with John Wayne.

I feel very strongly that the director is supposed to be the boss. Art was never created by democracy.
Charlton Heston.

Cinema is the director's medium. It is written even less than it is acted, but it is primarily the director's medium. There are films for which actors are required, although this is not true of all roles, by any means . . . but the absolutely indispensable creative presence is the director.
Charlton Heston.

Preston Sturges, director, to actor Joel McCrea:
What you do is very good, but have you ever seen a man sit down at a piano and play one note over and over again? And have you ever seen a great concert pianist like Rubinstein play? Well, have you noticed that he uses all the notes, all the colours, all the graduations? Well, that's my story.
Joel McCrea, replying:
The way I figure it, Preston, is that Rubinstein and those guys are looking for the one note – and I've already found it.

My favourite is the actor who can do nothing well. By that I mean one who has presence, authority and can attract attention without actually doing anything. I suppose I really mean control.
Alfred Hitchcock.

Brando was deeply rebellious against the bourgeois spirit, the over-ordering of life. Dean represented the release of anger against parents, resentment at the failure of parents to understand. Brando was happily arrogant, a free spirit. Dean was sad and sulky, you kept expecting him to cry. De Niro is a number of things all at once. There are lots of different people in him. He finds release and fulfilment in becoming other people. Picture after picture he gets deep into the thing. He's found his solution for living at a time like this in his work.
Elia Kazan.

Kazan is *very* good with actors – he was an actor at one time. And a lot of young directors really don't understand actors, how to work with them. They're into techniques, effects. But Kazan really knows. He's schooled. He's – as far as I'm concerned – the best schooling.
Robert de Niro.

We had a problem persuading Tony Curtis to get into women's clothing.
Billy Wilder, on 'Some Like It Hot'.

Anyone can remember lines, but it takes a real artist to come on the set and not know her lines and give the performance she did.
Billy Wilder, on Marilyn Monroe.

Directing her was like directing Lassie. You needed fourteen takes to get each one of them right.
Otto Preminger, on Marilyn Monroe.

I have never met anyone as utterly mean as Marilyn Monroe. Nor as utterly fabulous on the screen, and that includes Garbo.
Billy Wilder.

It used to be you'd call her at 9am, she'd show up at noon. Now you call her in May – she shows up in October. We should be able to kick out an actress, have Piper Laurie warming up, and get on with it.
Billy Wilder,
on Marilyn Monroe during the shooting of her last (uncompleted) film, 'Something's Got To Give'.

Audrey Hepburn is like a salmon swimming upstream. She can do it with very small bozooms. Titism has taken over this country. This girl single-handed may make bozooms a thing of the past. The director will not have to invent shots where the girl leans way forward for a glass of Scotch and soda.
Billy Wilder.

Marilyn Monroe was sensitive and very difficult. She tried hard, but you had to wait for her to come through, to start rolling, and then her kind of inhibition disappeared and after that she was phenomenal, one of the great comediennes.
Billy Wilder.

As near genius as any actress I ever knew.
Joshua Logan, on Marilyn Monroe.

When I first saw von Stroheim at the wardrobe tests for his role as Rommel (in 'Five Graves to Cairo'), I clicked my heels and said: 'Isn't it ridiculous, little me directing you? You were always ten years ahead of your time.' And he replied, 'Twenty.'
Billy Wilder.

I've never worked with an actor who was less conscious of his good image.
Don Siegel, on Clint Eastwood.

Sometimes an actor is intelligent enough to overcome his limitations and discover for himself the proper path to follow – that is, he uses his own intelligence . . . When this happens, he has the qualities of a director.
Michaelangelo Antonioni.

MICHAELANGELO ANTONIONI.

Creation must be total for the director from beginning to end. I'm convinced that the present failure of Hollywood is because of this. To divide, in art, is not to conquer.
Jean Renoir.

Anyone can direct a good picture if he's got a good script.
Garson Kanin.

He was the first to photograph thought.
Cecil B. de Mille, on D. W. Griffith.

I care nothing about the story, only how it is photographed and presented.
Josef von Sternberg.

When a director dies, he becomes a photographer.
John Grierson, on Josef von Sternberg.

He has no knowledge of camera direction. His films are completely theatre.
Karl Struss, on Chaplin.

I didn't write the Bible and I didn't invent sin.
Cecil B. de Mille.

A picture is made a success not on a set but over the drawing board.
Cecil B. de Mille.

The trouble with Cecil is that he always bites off more than he can chew – and then chews it.
William de Mille, on his brother.

I never met such an egotist in my life. Even if he was wrong and knew it, once he said it, it had to be.
Arthur Miller, on Cecil B. de Mille.

There was a time – only once – when de Mille decided to do a comedy, which could never have worked, because de Mille was a completely humourless man who took himself very seriously.
Robert Emmett Dolan.

Give me any two pages of the Bible and I'll give you a picture.
Cecil B. de Mille.

You can make a thousand movies out of one incident. What some people would call third-rate movies. I don't believe they're third-rate movies.
Martin Scorsese.

It's the Lubitsch touch that means so much.
Slogan on film posters, c.1925.

I sometimes make pictures that are not up to my standard, but then it can only be said of a mediocrity that all his work is up to his standard.
Ernst Lubitsch.

LEFT: ERNST LUBITSCH WITH CIGAR.

ROBERT DE NIRO WITH MARTIN SCORSESE.

Democracy is a fine way to run a country, but it's a hell of a way to make pictures.
Lillian Hellman,
after working with Marlon Brando and Arthur Penn on the Sam Spiegel production of 'The Chase'.

As a writer I never felt myself so completely identified with the picture as I did when I directed it. I suppose only the director feels the full, one hundred percent thrill of the movie maker. The picture is his own more than it belongs to any other single person of all the many who must collaborate in its production. He it is who takes all the materials – the story, the sets, the lights, the characters, the actors, the costumes, the make-ups, the properties, and moulds them moment by moment into the living thing which is a motion picture.
William de Mille.

If you want to become a director, you should sit on top of the camera and pant like a tiger.
Mike Curtiz, advice to prop man.

I have never been drawn to the whodunnit pure and simple: that's an intellectual exercise containing no emotion you see. Now suspense acts as a spur, and adventure involves audiences' emotions.
Alfred Hitchcock.

There is no terror in a bang, only in the anticipation of it.
Alfred Hitchcock.

There is no suspense like the suspense of a delayed coition.
D.W. Griffith.

When you decide to do a picture like that ('Taxi Driver'), you're going to have to go all the way. It's a picture of yourself up there and if they don't like it, they don't like you. You think maybe by doing it you will have worked it out of your system.
Martin Scorsese.

'Mean Streets' comes from my feelings, from myself, my own life, in a sense. People are always talking right on the edge of their emotions, always yelling. It's a way of life. The idea was never to build up to it . . . That's the way the characters live. That's the way I am.
Martin Scorsese.

Johnny, it's the usual slashed-wrist shot.
Billy Wilder,
to cameraman John Seitz when setting-up Gloria Swanson's attempted suicide in 'Sunset Boulevard'.

Johnny, it's the usual dead-chimpanzee set-up.
Billy Wilder,
to cameraman John Seitz while working on 'Sunset Boulevard'.

You'll be no good. You're not a bastard. To be a good director, you've got to be a bastard. I'm one, and I know it. Look at John Ford, or George Stevens, or Willie Wyler – all bastards! But I know you, Nunnally – you won't ever fight. Something comes up, you'll compromise.
Henry Hathaway,
advising Nunnally Johnson against becoming a director.

In one way it's very nice . . . but you know we can't go on forever and not tell our friends and relatives how we are earning our living.
D. W. Griffith.

Son, always give 'em a good show, and travel first class.
Walter Huston, to his son John.

Make 'em redecorate your office. That's primary – to make them know where you stand. Then, when you're shooting interior sequences, use your own interior decorator and set dresser. That way, everything on the set will fit your house when you're finished.
Blake Edwards,
advising George Axelrod on how to direct.

I've never made the film I wanted to make – no matter what happens, it never turns out exactly as I had hoped.
Roger Corman.

He was too large for this smelly resort, and the big studios were scared to death of him. A man who was a triple threat kept them awake nights, and I'm positive they were waiting for him to fall on his face so they could pounce and devour this terrible threat to their stingy talents . . . They pounced and they got him, good. But he knew the great days when his can glowed like a port light from their kissing it.
Earl Felton, on Preston Sturges.

When the last dime is gone, I'll sit on the curb outside with a pencil and a ten cent notebook, and start the whole thing over again.
Preston Sturges,
shortly before his Hollywood career came to an end.

A team effort is a lot of people doing what I say.
Michael Winner.

The best films are best because of nobody but the director.
Roman Polanski.

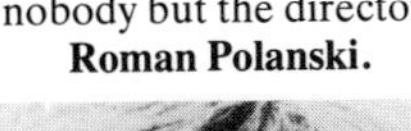

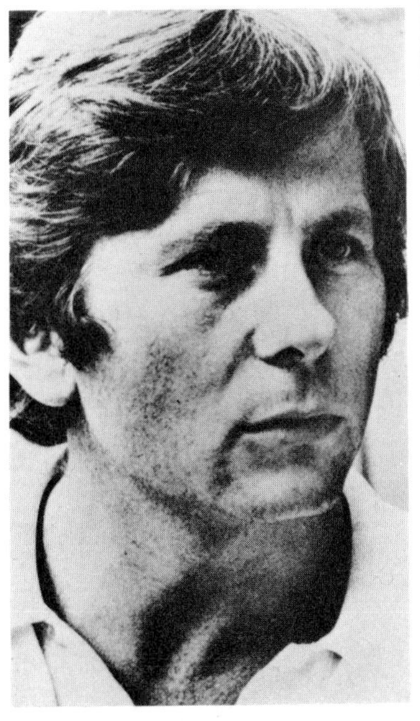

LEFT: WALTER HUSTON. RIGHT: ROMAN POLANSKI.

RIGHT: GEORGE CUKOR.

I'm interested in people, the way they behave. Other directors get their effects by showing doorknobs being turned, things like that. I like to concentrate on the actors' faces.
George Cukor.

Too many films are photos of people talking. Movies are meant to move and pieces of film should stick together to create ideas and emotion like words in a sentence.
Alfred Hitchcock.

Don't get excited. Obstacles make a better picture.
Victor Fleming.

You can have all the philosophy you like: if a film doesn't come across in graphic terms, it falls short.
Rouben Mamoulian.

The hardest part of directing is staying awake for nine weeks at a stretch.
Michael Winner.

I started at the top and worked down.
Orson Welles.

Everybody denies I am a genius – but nobody ever called me one.
Orson Welles.

An active loafer, a wise madman.
Jean Cocteau, on Orson Welles.

We were dealing with our own emotions. A lot of people's lives are soap operas; mine is anyway.
Martin Scorsese,
on 'Alice Doesn't Live Here Any More'.

I'm interested in the passions of people, man or woman.
Richard Brooks.

What influenced me most was an anecdote about D. W. Griffith. 'Move these 10,000 horses a trifle to the right,' he was quoted as saying in a grand manner to his assistant, who rushed to obey, while the master tried to breathe a little easier by removing some obstruction from his large nostrils. 'And that mob out there three feet forward' – this to another of his eager assistants, while his thumb was still in his nose. While his orders were being carried out he looked down benevolently at a small boy who had ventured admiringly to his side. 'Young man,' he said, 'when you grow up, would you like to be a director?' 'Naw', drawled the youngster, 'my father doesn't let me pick my nose.'
Josef von Sternberg.

Film-making has become a kind of hysterical pregnancy.
Richard Lester.

You watch, the new wave will discover the slow dissolve in ten years or so.
Billy Wilder, c. 1969.

I used to be prejudiced against directors, but now I'm bigoted against them.
Isobel Lennart.

In our marketing of American pictures the director's name has been so established in the minds of the public that he has become a major box-office asset for any picture he directs.
George Sidney, 1962.

Mike Nichols is the greatest director ever in films. Why? Because he never had a failure.
Joseph Levine.

PRESTON STURGES.

I think the pictures that have been made by directors who have become producer-directors are better on an average than they were when they worked solely as directors. I know it's a more satisfactory way of working. I like to consider myself a picture-maker more than a man who directs in the strict sense of the word . . . I like doing it by myself. If I'm wrong then I'd like to be totally responsible for being wrong.
Preston Sturges.

Since the director is the hub of the picture, there will always be difficulty if you have a creative producer unless there is tremendous teamwork and rapport. So by and large my feeling is that the emergence of the producer-director for top creative people has been a very wise thing.
Stanley Kramer.

I'd like to help to abolish the adage that you're only as good as your last picture.
Steven Spielberg.

We are all mendicants in the movies. To a certain extent we are standing with our hands out waiting for manna from heaven. Sometimes you shoot and see if God isn't going to put something on your plate. Sometimes he does – then you grab it.
Orson Welles.

The film industry is only a diverting entertainment for people in politics and business. In a way, I've always looked at movies as dessert, something to treat yourself to after a hard day at work or school . . . Movies might be my life, but it's not the way for 225 million other Americans. There's more to living than re-creating life on celluloid. This is something I'm beginning to find out.
Steven Spielberg.

Those were the days at Roach when some guy would come in and say, 'Listen – Laurel and Hardy in a cobbler's shop.' I'd say, 'Yes? Then what?' and the guy would say, 'That's it – take over.'
Leo McCarey,
on directing Hal Roach two-reelers.

You're all alone in this dim, dark, dank, dingy, ancient, oozing, slimy castle at four o'clock in the morning. Your mother's been carried off by the Frankenstein monster, your father's been killed by the wolf-man, the servants have fled, your lover is being chased across the moors by the dogs.I want to get the feeling from you, as you come down this stairway, that you're fed up with it all.
Direction to Evelyn Ankers
during the filming of 'The Ghost of Frankenstein'.

Almost always when I'm on set or on location I have music playing to try to make people think they are not making movies – in the ordinary sense of the word.
Orson Welles.

Johnny, keep it out of focus. I want to win the foreign picture award.
Billy Wilder,
to cameraman John Seitz during the shooting of 'Sunset Boulevard'.

There was this obnoxious little character – I think he was the son of some big shot. He said, 'You're way behind schedule.' He'd been pestering me for days, so I tore out ten pages of script and said. 'Now we're three days ahead of schedule. Are you happy?'
John Ford.

Sit a little more female.
Mike Curtiz, instruction to actress.

It is morning and a haystack and lots of sunlight – turn over on your stomach and look sex.
Mike Curtiz, instruction to actress.

'Shadows' was the first picture we saw that proved you could make a film . . . and keep making a film. First, get a camera, and move it.
Martin Scorsese.

If you're going to imitate – and I must say that one frankly must admit that you have to imitate in films – you may as well imitate the best.
Arthur Penn.

I always think of my style as a curious cross between Lubitsch and Stroheim.
Billy Wilder.

I felt the urge to direct because I couldn't stomach what was being done with what I wrote.
Joseph L. Mankiewicz.

When Alfred Hitchcock admitted to a top executive that he didn't see many pictures, the executive, in all seriousness, said, 'Then where do you get your ideas?'
Ken Englund.

Any American director who says he hasn't been influenced by him is out of his mind.
John Frankenheimer, on Alfred Hitchcock.

When you find out a thing goes pretty well, you might as well do it again.
Howard Hawks, on his cinematic style.

All a cutter had to do with Ford's takes was to cut off the slate number and put them together in sequence. This was Ford's guarantee against possible butchery by front-office executives or wandering meddlers. Ford left them no extra footage to fool around with.
Robert Parrish, on John Ford.

On a film set the only person less important than the director is a talent agent.
John Cassavetes.

I'm a whore. I go where I'm kicked. But I'm a very good whore.
Sam Peckinpah.

I am interested in failures – the homosexual genius, the suicidal genius, the fantasist genius, all these people are heroes to me.
Ken Russell.

They let the studio janitor cut 'The Magnificent Ambersons' in my absence.
Orson Welles.

Bring on the empty horses!
Michael Curtiz,
during location shooting for 'The Charge Of the Light Brigade'.

ERROL FLYNN IN 'THE CHARGE OF THE LIGHT BRIGADE'.

PAUL NEWMAN IN 'THE LEFT-HANDED GUN'

We felt we could begin to open up the western into the areas of human psychology which had always been there ever since the western was born, but had found relatively few outlets in western movies.
Arthur Penn,
on 'The Left-Handed Gun'.

Someone says in 'The Fortune Cookie', 'People will do anything for money. Except for some people. They will do *almost* anything for money.' I guess that's the theme of all my pictures. Maybe my philosophy is cynical, but I have to be true to what I feel.
Billy Wilder.

The close-up is such a valuable thing – like a trump at bridge.
Billy Wilder.

We can make bad pictures, too . . . Costs more, but we can make 'em.
John Huston.

The questions and feelings in Bergman's films are what interest me – an investigation of spiritual values and faith . . . The line between the kind of solemnity I want and comedy is very, very thin. That's why it's so easy to satirize Bergman . . . My biggest fear is that I'll write mawkish and embarrassing soap-opera and not know it.
Woody Allen.

I suppose it's because I was born with two crystal balls.
Alfred Hitchcock,
asked why he seemed consistently able to cast beautiful unknown actresses who later became stars.

Poe writes the first reel or the last reel. Roger does the rest.
James H. Nicholson on Roger Corman.

If I made 'Cinderella', the audience would be looking for the body in the coach.
Alfred Hitchcock.

One is imprisoned by suspense. Nobody would go and see a musical by me. So one feels limited. And one spends one's life avoiding the cliché – the one consolation being that self-plagiarism is style.
Alfred Hitchcock.

The task I'm trying to achieve above all is to make you see.
D. W. Griffith.

A film-maker isn't supposed to say things. He's supposed to show them.
Alfred Hitchcock.

Hitchcock's idea of characters is rather primitive.
Raymond Chandler.

The great art is contrivance. If you take adventure films, character as such plays no part really. The trick is to get the characters on the move, on the run. Too many devices have to be used if you analyse character.
Alfred Hitchcock.

It's worth a lot more than money to be working for me.
D. W. Griffith,
replying to an actor's request for a raise.

Always make an audience suffer as much as possible.
Alfred Hitchcock.

Writers are the only ones who can express their ego. Directors can't because they have to please the majority. We can't deal with opinions. All we can do is to weave a little romance as pleasantly as we know how.
D. W. Griffith.

He never once looked in the camera when we worked together. You see the man had bad eyes, as long as I knew him, but he was a man whose veins ran with the business.
Arthur Miller
(the cinematographer), on John Ford.

There is a certain attempt on my part to unsettle the audience, really. To catch them as unaware as the characters in the film are being caught unaware . . . Very early on, as I watch a film, I feel that I know just what it is going to be about – I know where it's going to get to eventually. And I'd rather that should not be so in my films.
Arthur Penn.

I would not repeat myself. The studio will because they're in the business to make money. They gamble on people more than scripts because who knows what will capture the public's imagination. I don't, and I make 'em. All I can do is make stories I become involved with.
Norman Jewison.

I've always felt I was indictable as a film-maker on the basis of triviality. That's my own biggest self-criticism and one that I accept unhesitatingly from anyone who wants to level it.
Woody Allen.

You make just one good picture and nobody will ever remember the other guy.
Anonymous studio executive,
advising Elia Kazan to change his name to 'Cézanne'.

The best directing is the one you don't see.
Billy Wilder.

There is not a man working in movies, nor a man who cares for them, who does not owe Griffith more than he owes anyone else.
James Agee.

I have ten commandments. The first nine are 'Thou shalt not bore'. The tenth is 'Thou shalt have the right of final cut.'
Billy Wilder.

His tragedy is that of the innovator who has run out of innovations.
Andrew Sarris, on Rouben Mamoulian.

Editing is a characteristic that I don't think you can distinguish from the rest of the direction.
Arthur Penn.

He has such verve. We can use his body.
D. W. Griffith,
on Douglas Fairbanks, Sr.

If you get your head above the mob, they try to knock it off. If you stay down, you last forever.
Allan Dwan.

You are here to please me. Nothing else on earth matters.
Cecil B. de Mille, to his staff.

There, but for the grace of God, goes God.
Herman Mankiewicz, of Orson Welles.

My personality is that of an egotistical adventurer.
Orson Welles.

ORSON WELLES AS 'CITIZEN KANE'

Chapter 7

Write And Wrong

The writer is a necessary evil.
Irving Thalberg.

There was a law in the studios – hire only the best. As a result, the writer who had written well in some other medium was paid the most. His task was *not* to write as well for the movies. His large salary was a bribe.
Ben Hecht, 1957.

If there was any truth in the original it had been carefully altered. If anything had been left unchanged it was because it was untrue.
Graham Greene, on 'Orient Express', the film version of his book 'Stamboul Train'.

They ruin your stories. They massacre your ideas. They prostitute your art. They trample on your pride. And what do you get for it? A fortune.
Unnamed screenwriter.

Never let that bastard back in here – unless we need him.
Variously attributed to L. B. Mayer, Harry Cohn, Jack L. Warner, Harry M. Warner, Sam Goldwyn and Adolph Zukor, after dismissing a troublesome writer.

Writers clutter up a story conference.
Eddie Mannix.

I want to know one thing – just what was the motivation of the man-eating tiger?
Unnamed producer, during a script conference on a jungle picture.

I feel the first draft of a script should be done by the writer, completely independent of anyone once the subject matter is agreed upon. That's how they get the most from me. I have had my say, now I'm wide open to suggestions.
Dalton Trumbo.

I'm afraid I lean on a script, and probably that's where my mark gets left for better or worse, probably with varying responses from the authors depending on how intruded upon they feel . . . I do very little makeshift work on the set. I like to go in with a strong script and adhere to it pretty closely.
Arthur Penn.

The basic art of motion pictures is the screenplay; it is fundamental, without it there is nothing.
Raymond Chandler.

You can't stick to the written word when a scene is transformed unpredictably just by the look of a particular actor or the way the setting fits around the camera.
John Boorman.

The system under which writers work in Hollywood would sap the vitality of a Shakespeare. They are intelligent enough to know that they are writing trash, but they are not intelligent enough to do anything about it.
Dalton Trumbo.

'Well . . . how is it coming?' . . . has been the standard greeting to screenwriters throughout the ages, spoken always in a suspicious, accusing tone of voice.
Ken Englund.

What I have crossed out I didn't like. What I haven't crossed out I am dissatisfied with.
Cecil B. de Mille, returning a writer's script.

Take out the essentials and what have you got?
MGM executive's typical comment when assessing script ideas.

Since arriving, I have written four versions of 'Abraham Lincoln', including a good one, playable in their required time. That, of course, is out. Seven people, including myself, are now working in conferences on the fifth one which promises to be the worst yet. If I don't get out of here soon I am going crazy. Perhaps I am crazy now. I wouldn't be surprised.
Stephen Vincent Benét.

Charlie (MacArthur) and I worked together in Hollywood on many scripts. We had the same opinions, although we expressed them differently. I was for broadcasting mine. Charlie said, 'Complaints are only a sign that you've been hurt. Keep the wounds out of sight.' We argued this point from our earliest meetings. Once, in a speakeasy, Dorothy Parker quoted Hemingway's line that 'courage is grace under pressure.' I dissented. Charlie agreed. 'That's posing for others,' I said. Charlie said, 'It's posing for yourself.'
Ben Hecht.

It was said that if anyone could sign his name to a contract he was sure of an annual salary of at least 100,000 dollars – for two weeks.
Marc Connelly, on the 'Hollywood writing rush' of the 20's and 30's.

I want this to be the story of a typical American family. Just simple, ordinary people, the kind you meet every day on the street. Typical, see – the father makes about twenty thousand a year.
Unnamed MGM producer, instructing two writers, c. 1935.

It's just a damn good hot-tale, so don't get a lot of thees and thous and thums on your mind.
Cecil B. de Mille, to a writer working on one of his biblical epics.

'Where's the menace?: Where is the menace? I can answer that very simply. You are the menace.
George Middleton, playwright, to Fox producer Sol Wurtzel, after Wurtzel kept demanding a Middleton script.

It's a terrible thing to say, but I can't think of good women writers. Of course, calling them women writers is their ruin; they begin to think of themselves that way.
Dorothy Parker.

The boss who hired Dostoyevski to write like Horatio Alger somehow became Feodor's superior.
Ben Hecht.

You call this a script? Give me a couple of 5000-dollar-a-week writers and I'll write it myself.
Joe Pasternak.

Writing cheaply, writing falsely, writing with 'less' than you have, is a painful thing. To betray belief is to feel sinful, guilty – and taste bad. Nor is movie writing easier than good writing. It's just as hard to make a toilet seat as it is a castle window. But the view is different.
Ben Hecht.

Try to find out who the star of your film will actually be. It's very disconcerting to have written something for Joan Crawford and find it's Lana Turner who'll be the actual star. Secondly, never tackle a screenplay at the beginning of its development. Let the producer and his other writers mess it up and then, when they're faced with an actual shooting date, you do the final job. And finally, you must learn not to let them break your heart.
Donald Ogden Stewart, advice to screenwriters.

When Jack Warner hired him to write scripts at the studio, Mizner came into Warner's office with the Los Angeles telephone book, dropped it on his desk and said, 'This might have been good for a picture – except it has too many characters in it.'
Joseph L. Mankiewicz.

Unnamed successful screenwriter, questioning the existence of a stratum of low paid Hollywood writers – the so-called '75-dollar-a-week writers' – during a Screen Writers' Guild meeting:
Tell me, do you know any 75-dollar-a-week writers?

Herman Mankiewicz, replying;
I know lots of them, but they're all making 1500 dollars a week.

It took me fifteen years to discover that I had no talent for writing, but I couldn't give it up because by that time I was too famous.
Robert Benchley.

ROBERT BENCHLEY.

I know less about writing than you do. But so does the audience. My tastes are exactly those of the audience. What I don't like, the audience won't like.
Unnamed Hollywood boss, to Charles MacArthur.

I do most of my work sitting down. That's where I shine.
Robert Benchley.

Being a good writer is no feather bed. Writing is almost as lonely a craft as flagpole sitting (and is becoming almost as passé). You write behind a closed door, and fun is your enemy.
Ben Hecht.

The biggest obstacle to professional writing today is the necessity for changing the typewriter ribbon.
Robert Benchley.

Well, when we sell a story to the studio, we take the cheque and kiss the story goodbye. And maybe months and months, or a year later when we hear that a certain story that smells like it, was that one is being previewed, well, we run to the preview and see what the hell they've done with it.
Percy Heath, 1929.

It was the credo that finally landed Hollywood in the dustbin. But when movies were the only toy on the market, it was the Eleventh Commandment – 'Write down.'
Ben Hecht, 1957.

A writer who goes over a fifteen-thousand-dollar yearly budget has to serve other than Art. The figure may be a little high for the poet, but who considers the poets? Plato long ago threw them out of any ideal republic.
Ben Hecht, 1957.

Let me tell you about writing for films. You finish your book. Now, you know where the California state line is? Well, you drive right up to that line, take your manuscript and pitch it across. No, on second thoughts, don't pitch it across. First, let them toss the money over. *Then* you throw it over, pick up the money and get the hell out of there.
Ernest Hemingway.

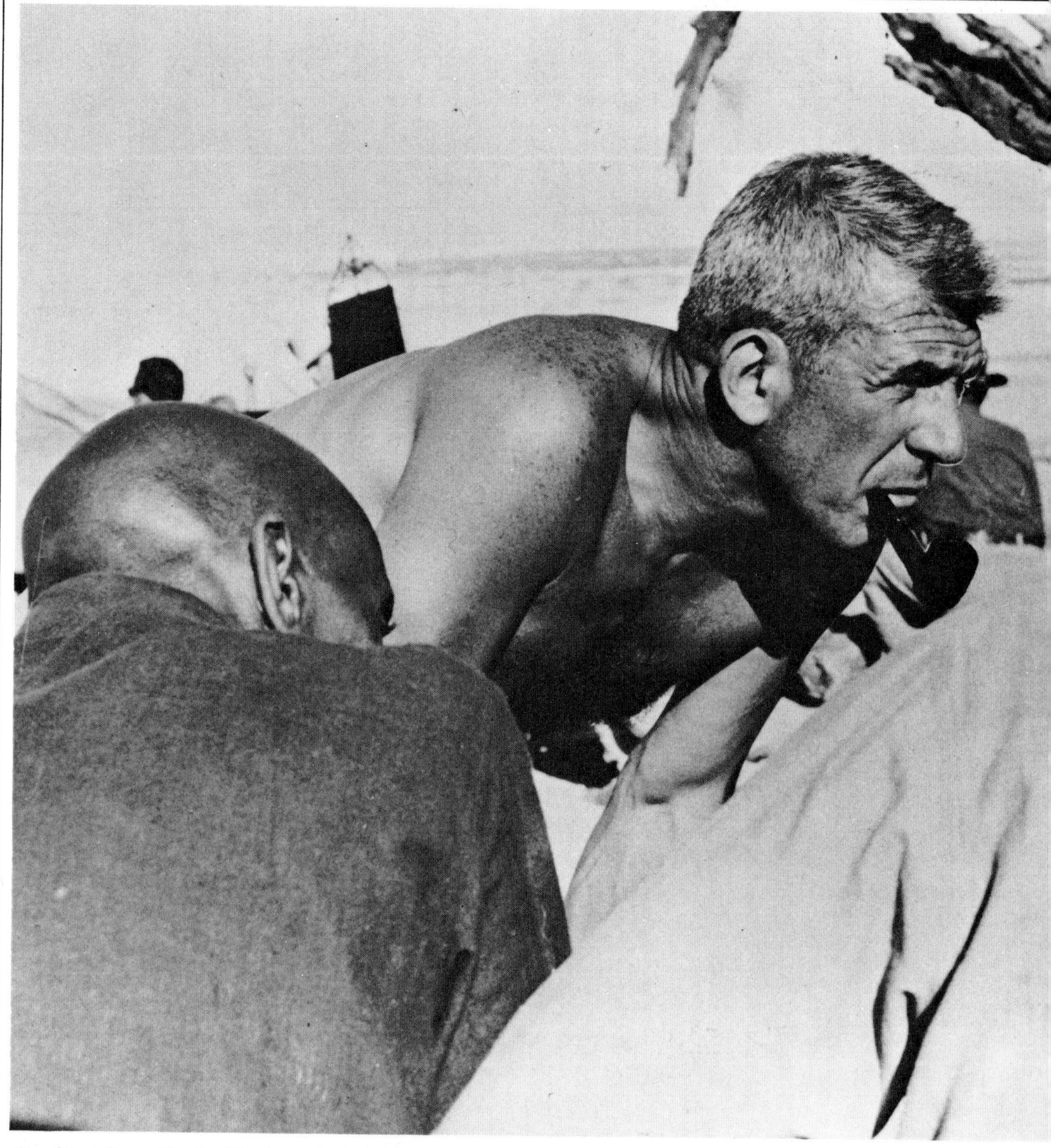

RICHARD BROOKS ON LOCATION FOR 'THE PROFESSIONALS'.

Ben (Hecht) and Charlie (MacArthur) did . . . the script for 'Wuthering Heights' in two weeks flat, for Walter Wanger . . . They didn't bother too much with the Brontë book – they did it from an outline. Wanger sold it to Sam Goldwyn, and Sam made it into a big hit. Ben was always good at pressure jobs. He worked on 'Gone With the Wind' for David Selznick – never read that, either. Claimed reading the book would only confuse him, and you know, maybe he was right?

Leland Hayward.

Twenty-seven words, all bad.

Edward Albee,
author, on Ernest Lehmann's screen adaptation of his play 'Who's Afraid of Virginia Woolf' (Lehmann, such was his respect for Albee, had left the original almost unchanged).

I remember we bought 'The Moon is Down', which was on the stage in New York, and when I said, 'Look have you got any suggestions?' Steinbeck (who was the author) said, 'Yeah, tamper with it.'

Nunnally Johnson.

If there's anything I know it's the sound of how my generation has spoken. I've listened to its dialogue for twenty years. I've done little else with my life than listen to it speak.

F. Scott Fitzgerald,
to an unnamed studio boss who had rewritten one of his scripts.

I got a call one day from Metro. They were completely confused over there and they wanted to know where in hell was my client, (William) Faulkner! They were pretty sore – nobody was supposed to walk out of Metro without letting the front office know where he'd gone. I didn't know where Bill was. He hadn't told me he was going anywhere. I got the office to start making calls all over the damned place, and finally we thought of trying him at his home in Mississippi, and sure enough, there he was. 'What the hell are you doing down there?' I yelled on the phone, and he said, 'Well, ah asked my producer if ah could work at home, and he said fine, so heah ah am.'

Leland Hayward.

Every screenwriter worthy of the name has already directed his film when he has written his script.

Joseph L. Mankiewicz.

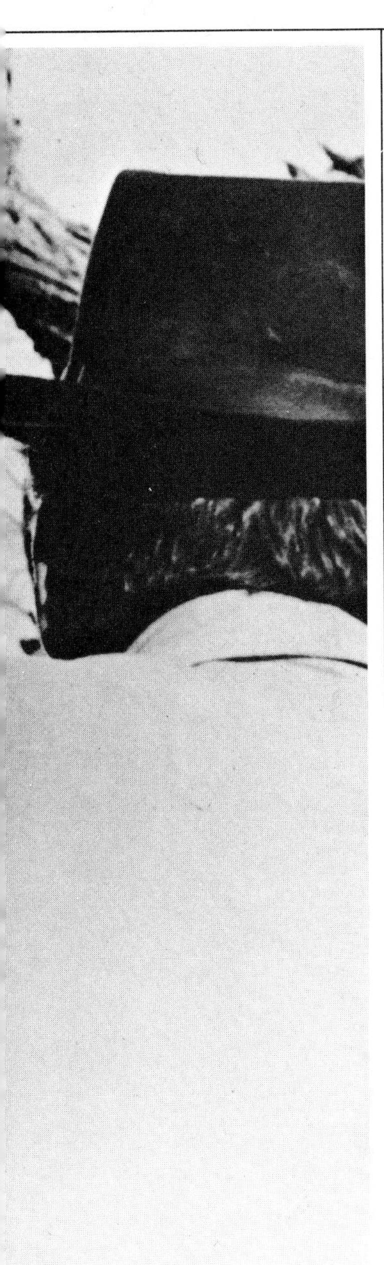

Any *good* writer, to write a woman, must be able to have some woman in him.
Richard Brooks.

Writing a good movie brings a writer about as much fame as riding a bicycle.
Ben Hecht.

You can make a good picture out of it and I hope you do, but my statement remains right here in the book, that's all.
John Steinbeck,
to Nunnally Johnson who wrote the screenplay for 'The Grapes of Wrath'.

I venture to say that out here in this whole town there are only three writers who can do a script alone – Shavelson and Rose, the Hacketts, and the Epstein brothers.
Jerry Wald.

Each book purchased for motion pictures has some individual quality, good or bad, that has made it remarkable. It is the work of a great array of highly paid and incompatible writers to distinguish this quality, separate it, and obliterate it.
Evelyn Waugh.

In Hollywood we acquire the finest novels in order to smell the leather bindings.
Ernst Lubitsch.

All good writing is swimming under water and holding your breath.
F. Scott Fitzgerald.

Show me a hero and I will write you a tragedy.
F. Scott Fitzgerald.

I am a camera with its shutter open, quite passive, recording, not thinking.
Christopher Isherwood, 'The Berlin Stories'.

It is the writer's privilege to help man endure by lifting his heart.
William Faulkner.

The writer's only responsibility is to his art. He will be completely ruthless if he is a good one. He has a dream. It anguishes him so much that he must get rid of it. He has no peace until then . . . If a writer has to rob his mother, he will not hesitate; the 'Ode to a Grecian Urn' is worth any number of old ladies.
William Faulkner.

Jesus Christ, it ain't possible!
William Faulkner.
His verdict after ten minutes exposure to a typical MGM production at a private viewing arranged by Irving Thalberg.

When I take up streetwalking, the street will be Broadway, not Hollywood Boulevard.
Alexander Woollcott,
on being told he could earn 1000 dollars a week writing for films.

When in doubt, have two guys come through the door with guns in their fists.
Raymond Chandler.

If the writer is too exact in defining every move of the camera, every cut and angle, he robs the director of freedom in his own proper field; he ties the director's hands to the point of cramping his cinematic style and preventing his use of the camera as an instrument for emphasising dramatic values instead of merely recording action.
William de Mille.

If my books had been any worse I would not have been invited to Hollywood. If they had been any better I would not have come.
Raymond Chandler.

In the making of a picture, the fellow most unappreciated by the man who wrote the original material is the writer of the screenplay. I must have done a hundred pictures and I don't suppose there's ten men or maybe five who remained a friend or indicated in any way that they forgave me or cared for it.
Nunnally Johnson.

He thought screenwriting was one of the hardest jobs in the world, said he could never do it. He never did, either. Best I ever got out of him were occasional lines of dialogue. The rest, I assure you, I stole hook, line and sinker from his stories. He used to wonder how I could imitate him so well. I wasn't imitating him at all; I was stealing his own sentence structure and phrases right and left. He used to say . . . that screenwriting was a special kind of job; it required being a novelist, a playwright, and a civil engineer. Maybe it's because he was a writer himself, but he believed that the story was the most important part of the film, but that you could make a good screenplay out of a bad story.
Leonard Spigelgass, on Damon Runyon.

When you steal from one author, it's plagiarism; if you steal from many, it's research.
Wilson Mizner.

WILSON MIZNER.

Chapter 8

Public Eye

I think I appeal to the escapism in people – the characters I play, let me put it that way. I like those characters myself. That's why, maybe, I carry them to other extremes than my predecessors.
Clint Eastwood.

I make pictures for people, not for critics.
Cecil B. de Mille.

The only thing you owe the public is a good performance.
Humphrey Bogart.

There is only one thing that can kill the movies, and that is education.
Will Rogers.

I let the audience use their imaginations. Can I help it if they misconstrue my suggestions?
Ernst Lubitsch.

Whether the movies imitate life or whether life imitates the movies is for others to decide . . . Some critics say that audiences complain about the movies because the movies do not reflect reality; it is this writer's suspicion that more people lament the fact that reality does not reflect the movies.
Leo Rosten.

The kind of jackass who likes the movies as they are is the man who keeps them as they are.
H. L. Mencken.

I know audiences feed on crap, but I cannot believe we are so lacking that we cannot dish it up to them with some trace of originality.
Darryl F. Zanuck.

Tell me, why did you stop writing?
Charlie Chaplin,
to comedian Jackie Vernon, on their first meeting (years earlier, Vernon, as a child, had directed a steady stream of letters at Chaplin, his idol, without receiving a single reply).

Go away, go away! I don't need you anymore.
Norma Talmadge,
to autograph hunters after her retirement.

The only reason they come to see me is that I know life is great – and they know I know it.
Clark Gable.

The public has always expected me to be a playboy, and a decent chap never lets his public down.
Errol Flynn.

To the Walter Mittys of the world he was all the heroes in one magnificent, sexy, animal package.
Jack L. Warner, on Errol Flynn.

Sticks Nix Hicks Pix
'Variety' headline
credited to the editor, Sime Silverman.

The popularity of motion pictures (which are a natural form of dramatic expression) will ride higher and higher as the quality of motion pictures rises higher and higher.
D.W. Griffith, 1924.

Hollywood is the worst of the dope peddlers because it sells its opium under a false label. Its customers pull at the pipe in the belief that it is harmless and, when finally they give it up, find that they are still helplessly dreaming the former delusions.
George Jean Nathan, 1949.

The avoidance of any obligation or accountability goes hand in hand with Hollywood's stubborn belief that the mind of the average American film-goer is that of a twelve-year-old child.
William Fadiman.

The public is never wrong.
Adolph Zukor.

Busy yourselves with that, you damned walruses, while the rest of us proceed with the play.
John Barrymore,
throwing a fish at a coughing audience.

You can't spring a new plot on an audience the first time and expect it to go. It takes a movie audience years to get used to a new plot.
Will Rogers.

I don't try to guess what a million people will like. It's hard enough to know what I like.
John Huston.

The most beautiful thing of all is the complete stillness of an audience so intent that it hardly breathes.
Charles Laughton.

Every now and then, when you're on stage, you hear the best sound a player can hear. It's a sound you can't get in movies or television. It is the sound of a wonderful, deep silence that means you've hit them where they live.
Shelley Winters.

Fans are people who let an actor know he's not alone in the way he feels about himself.
Anonymous.

Public taste is an ascending spiral.
Darryl F. Zanuck.

People ask me 'how come you been around so long?' Well, it's through playing the part of Mr. Average Joe American.
Gary Cooper.

GARY COOPER IN 'HIGH NOON'.

LEFT: CLINT EASTWOOD.

Chapter 9

Bouquets And Brickbats

LEFT: GEORGE RAFT. RIGHT: W. C. FIELDS.

TOM MIX.

They say he rides like part of the horse, but they don't say what part.
Robert Sherwood, on Tom Mix.

It took longer to make one of Mary's contracts than it did to make one of her pictures.
Sam Goldwyn, on Mary Pickford.

That obstinate, suspicious, egocentric, maddening and lovable genius of a problem child.
Mary Pickford, on Charlie Chaplin.

When he found a voice to say what was on his mind, he was like a child of eight writing lyrics for Beethoven's Ninth.
Billy Wilder, on Charlie Chaplin.

Chaplin is no business man – all he knows is that he can't take anything less.
Sam Goldwyn.

The public doesn't line up outside the box office when your name appears as they do for mine.
Charlie Chaplin, to Mack Sennett.

At a difficult period in American history, Douglas Fairbanks appeared to know all the answers.
Alistair Cooke.

With the release of 'Casablanca', Humphrey Bogart became big business. It was time for Lauren Bacall, who was primarily a business woman, to make her entrance. She, who was also to become his perfect screen partner, as seductive as Eve, as cool as the serpent.
Louise Brooks.

She makes dialogue sound better than it is by a matchless clarity and beauty of diction and by a fineness of intelligence and sensibility that illuminates every shade of meaning in every line she speaks.
Tennessee Williams, on Katharine Hepburn.

He moved through a movie scene like an exquisite paper knife.
Heywood Broun, on John Barrymore.

Marion Davies! I have yet to encounter a single movie fan with the slightest respect for her ability – and yet the coal that has been used to keep her name flaming on the electric signs would probably run the city of Syracuse for a whole year.
Sherwood Anderson.

Bogart's a hell of a nice guy till 11.30 pm. After that he thinks he's Bogart.
Dave Chasen.

A poet of the real.
Clifford Odets, on Gary Cooper.

One of the most beloved illiterates this country has ever known.
Carl Sandburg, on Gary Cooper.

When he puts his arms around me, I feel like a horse.
Clara Bow, on Gary Cooper.

Katharine Hepburn,
sighing with relief after finishing shooting 'A Bill of Divorcement' with John Barrymore: Thank goodness I don't have to act with you any more.
John Barrymore, replying:
I didn't know you ever had, darling.

She is a ten-year-old girl who has put on her mother's dress – and has done it convincingly.
Douglas Fairbanks Jr., on Joan Crawford.

He's a writer for the ages – for the ages of four to eight.
Dorothy Parker,
on an unnamed writer whom she considered overrated.

Massey won't be satisfied until he's assassinated.
George S. Kaufman,
on Raymond Massey, whose title role in 'Abe Lincoln in Illinois' (1939) was much applauded.

Joan Crawford was one of the people that made Hollywood the place that touched the imagination of the world.
George Cukor.

A wonderful instrument.
Rouben Mamoulian, on Greta Garbo.

Garbo's temperament reflected the rain and gloom of the long dark Swedish winters.
Lillian Gish.

What when drunk one sees in other women, one sees in Garbo sober.
Kenneth Tynan.

A deer in the body of a woman, living resentfully in the Hollywood zoo.
Clare Booth Luce, on Greta Garbo.

Co-starring with Garbo hardly constituted an introduction.
Fredric March.

I can't bear fools. **Dorothy Parker,** replying: That's queer, your mother could.
Anonymous date
of Dorothy Parker's, sneering at an amusing dinner guest.

His ears make him look like a taxicab with both doors open.
Howard Hughes, on Clark Gable.

The best ears of our lives.
Milton Berle, on Clark Gable.

He got a reputation as a great actor just by thinking hard about the next line.
King Vidor, on Gary Cooper.

Surely no-one but a mother could have loved Bette Davis at the height of her career.
Brian Aherne.

There were three things that Chico was always on – a phone, a horse or a broad.
Groucho Marx.

He was playing Bogart all the time, but he was really just a big sloppy bowl of mush.
Stanley Kramer.

Marilyn Monroe is a natural phenomenon like Niagara Falls or the Grand Canyon. You can't talk to it. It can't talk to you. All you can do is stand back and be awed by it.
Nunnally Johnson.

She knows the world, but this knowledge has now lowered her great and benevolent dignity; its darkness has not dimmed her goodness.
Edith Sitwell, on Marilyn Monroe.

Marilyn Monroe was a professional amateur.
Laurence Olivier.

I think Marilyn was as mad as a hatter.
Tony Curtis, on Marilyn Monroe.

Arsenic on the outside, a peach underneath.
Howard Dietz, on Alexander Woollcott.

The New Jersey Nero who mistakes his pinafore for a toga.
Edna Ferber, on Alexander Woollcott.

A fat duchess with the emotions of a fish.
Harold Ross, on Alexander Woollcott.

I think your slogan 'Liberty or Death' is splendid and whichever one you decide on will be all right with me.
Alexander Woollcott,
to the editor of 'New Yorker' magazine, Harold Ross.

The smartest of Alecs.
Heywood Broun, on Alexander Woollcott.

A pernickety fellow with more fizz than brain.
Ben Hecht, on Alexander Woollcott.

He loved the pure existence part of living, the yapping, scrapping, laughing, eating, romping, exploring the world part of it – but never, sad to say, the intimate, sexual part of it.
Harpo Marx, on Alexander Woollcott.

Improbable.
George S. Kaufman, on Alexander Woollcott.

Sorry I can't save your face if only for some museum.
Alexander Woollcott.
Telegram from him to Harold Ross, after Ross had asked Woollcott to delete part of a possibly libellous article.

I want to be alone on this trip. I don't expect to talk to a man or woman – just Alec Woollcott.
Edna Ferber,
before leaving for Europe.

My friends will tell you that Woollcott is a nasty old snipe. Don't believe them. Woollcott's friends are a pack of simps who move their lips when they read.
Alexander Woollcott.

I can't remember your name, but don't tell me.
Alexander Woollcott,
to an old college friend at a class reunion.

A combination of Little Nell and Lady Macbeth.
Alexander Woollcott, on Dorothy Parker.

Arlen, for all his reputation, is not a bounder. He is every other inch a gentleman.
Alexander Woollcott, on Michael Arlen.

Scrofulous with mica.
Alexander Woollcott,
of a woman overdressed in a spangled gown.

She ran the whole gamut of emotions from A to B.
Dorothy Parker,
on a performance by Katharine Hepburn.

Whenever I meet one of those Britishers I feel as if I have a papoose on my back.
Dorothy Parker.

How can you tell?
Dorothy Parker,
on hearing that Calvin Coolidge had died.

Excuse me, I just thought you were a fellow I once knew in Pittsburgh.
Groucho Marx,
who had just removed Greta Garbo's hat to see who she was.

THE MARX BROTHERS.

I don't want to be thought of as wholesome.
Julie Andrews, 1966.

She has that wonderful British strength that makes you wonder why they lost India.
Moss Hart, on Julie Andrews.

Working with her is like being hit over the head with a Valentine's card.
Christopher Plummer,
after filming 'The Sound of Music' with Julie Andrews.

If I were a man that's the girl I'd want to marry.
Jane Fonda, on Vanessa Redgrave.

Yes, but do we need another Burt Lancaster?
Hal Wallis,
on being told that new discovery Charlton Heston was 'another Burt Lancaster'.

Don't be hard on her. 'Funny Girl' is the first picture Miss Streisand's ever directed.
A friend to William Wyler – the director of 'Funny Girl'.

He has so many of his pictures being shown on the Late Show, he keeps more people up than Mexican food.
Hal Kanter, of Jimmy Stewart.

My impressions of Hank are of a man reaching but unreachable, gentle but capable of sudden wild and dangerous violence, sharply critical of others but equally self-critical, caged and fighting the bars but timid of the light, viciously opposed to external restraint, imposing an iron slavery on himself. His face is a picture of opposites in conflict.
John Steinbeck, on Henry Fonda.

When a legend grows up around a man there is often no means of pruning it, even within his family.
Jane Fonda, on her father Henry.

I've been in Volkswagens smaller than she was.
Harry Kurnitz, on an unnamed lover.

Let's face it, Billy Wilder at work is two people – Mr. Hyde and Mr. Hyde.
Harry Kurnitz.

Don't look now. Tallulah, but your show's slipping.
Heywood Broun,
to Tallulah Bankhead while she was starring in a Broadway show.

He is the Jewish Onassis of Beverly Hills – the only man to ride down Wilshire Boulevard in a yacht.
Oscar Levant, on the successful agent Irving Lazar.

I'm a controversial figure. My friends either dislike me or hate me.
Oscar Levant.

All done up like a well-kept grave.
W. C. Fields.

I am delighted to be here to pay tribute to Victor Saville, who is leaving for India – for 'Kim'.
Cedric Hardwicke,
at a farewell dinner for the director of 'Kim'.

Mr. Cobb took me into his library and showed me his books, of which he has a complete set.
Ring Larder,
after interviewing Irving Cobb.

She looked as though butter wouldn't melt in her mouth – or anywhere else.
Elsa Lanchester, on Maureen O'Hara.

Clare Booth Luce,
to Dorothy Parker as they stood together in front of the same door:
Age before beauty.
Dorothy Parker,
countering as she swept forward:
Pearls before swine.

Dear Mary, we all knew you had it in you.
Dorothy Parker.
Telegram sent by her to Mary Sherwood (wife of playwright Robert Sherwood) on the much-advertised birth of her child.

People who haven't talked to each other in years are on speaking terms again today – including the bride and groom.
Dorothy Parker,
on the occasion of her re-marriage to Alan Campbell.

That woman speaks eighteen languages and can't say 'No' in any of them.
Dorothy Parker,
on a guest at one of her parties.

Don't worry, if you keep him long enough he'll come back in style.
Dorothy Parker,
to a woman who had claimed a certain success in keeping her husband for seven years.

Probably sliding down a barrister.
Dorothy Parker,
on actress who had reportedly broken her leg while on holiday in London:

Outspoken by whom?
Dorothy Parker,
on a verbose and boorish show-biz party hostess who had been politely described as 'outspoken':

And where does she find them?
Dorothy Parker,
when informed that Clare Booth Luce was always kind to her inferiors:

If you don't mind my saying so, I think you're full of skit.
Dorothy Parker,
to an actor, recently returned from London, who was affecting the use of British forms of speech; including the 'soft' pronunciation of the word 'schedule':

A list of our authors who have made themselves most beloved and, therefore, most comfortable financially, shows that it is our national joy to mistake for the first rate, the fecund rate.
Dorothy Parker.

'And what sex, may I ask, is the mother?
Dorothy Parker,
on being told that a well-known transexual was going to visit the States to see her mother.

Jane has survived more bad movies than any actress should be able to in a lifetime.
Henry Fonda, on his daughter.

If she had nothing but her voice, she could break your heart with it. But she also had that beautiful body and the timeless loveliness of her face.
Ernest Hemingway, on Marlene Dietrich.

JULIE ANDREWS.

CENTRE: ELSA LANCHESTER.

Cagney's swift dialogue and swift movements had the glitter and precision of a meat-slicer.
Louise Brooks.

You have Van Gogh's ear for music.
Billy Wilder, to Cliff Osmond at an audition.

Say anything you like, but don't say I love to work. That sounds like Mary Pickford, the prissy bitch.
Mabel Normand, to the press.

Like kissing Hitler.
Tony Curtis, on Marilyn Monroe.

She's one of the finest women who ever walked the streets.
Mae West.

That man is so bad, he shouldn't be left alone in a room with a typewriter.
Herman Mankiewicz, on an unnamed scriptwriter.

You, Hyman, are the asbestos curtain between the audience and entertainment.
Bob Hopkins, to producer Bernie Hyman.

When he laughed, dust came out of his mouth.
Keenan Wynn, on an anonymous MGM producer.

You digger in the garbage of literature! . . . You impudent red-headed cur! You porter in the bawdy-house of words . . . You low rat. You befouler of the great dead. You slime of the underworld. You shady reprehensible rogue . . . You a better writer than O. Henry! Why, you couldn't sign his tax receipts! You're as illiterate as a publisher. If you had a Roman nose you'd be a courtesan . . . you damned brainless jazzer of decent English.
Wilson Mizner,
to Jim Tully after Tully claimed to be a better writer than O. Henry.

Alison Skipworth,
upset that Mae West seemed to be stealing a scene from her:
I'll have you know I'm an actress.
Mae West replying:
It's all right, dearie, I'll keep your secret.

I've seen 'A Night at the Opera' seventeen times . . . I just couldn't get over that love story between Allan Jones and Kitty Carlisle.
Mike Nichols,
to Groucho Marx on the occasion of their first meeting.

I never forget a face, but in your case I'll make an exception.
Groucho Marx.

She stole everything but the cameras.
George Raft,
on Mae West's debut film appearance.

CALVIN COOLIDGE.

Like cutting Tolstoy's beard so he wouldn't write any revolutionary novels.
Lionel Barrymore,
on hearing that L. B. Mayer had 'punished' Garbo for rejecting a story by casting her in a low budget western.

A square shooter if ever there awas one.
Spencer Tracy, on Jean Harlow.

She danced even when her feet were not moving.
Adolph Zukor, on Clara Bow.

He can give the audience pleasure just by walking across the floor.
Gene Kelly, on Fred Astaire.

I can't imagine any guy giving her a tumble.
Carl Laemmle, on Bette Davis.

He laughed until you could hear a pin drop.
Ring Lardner, on President Calvin Coolidge.

She's the original good time who was had by all.
Bette Davis, on an unnamed starlet.

Noel Coward,
as Edna Ferber arrived at the Algonquin Hotel wearing a trouser-suit:
My God, Edna, you look almost like a man.
Edna Ferber, replying:
So do you.

Two profiles pasted together.
Dorothy Parker, on Basil Rathbone.

Wet she was a star.
Joe Pasternak, on Esther Williams.

Chapter 10

Politics–The Spectre Haunting Hollywood

CENTRE: BILLY WILDER.

Nobody need worry any more that Washington is going left. Indeed, nobody need worry that the Washington of today is going anywhere.
Heywood Broun, 1935.

Are you now or have you ever been a member of the Communist Party?
J. Parnell Thomas.
Standard question from the House Un-American Activities Committee under **J. Parnell Thomas** to 'witnesses' from the film industry.

The more McCarthy yells, the better I like him. He's doing a job to get rid of the termites eating away at our democracy. I don't care how many toes he steps on, including mine, as long as he gets the job done. I hope he drives all the bums back to Moscow.
Louis B. Mayer (who was born in Minsk).

I can't for the life of me figure where men could get together and try in any form, shape or manner to deprive a man of a livelihood because of his political beliefs.
Jack Warner.

The Communists hate and fear the American motion picture. It is their number one hate.
Eric Johnston.

Hollywood is one of the main centres of Communist activity in America.
Adolphe Menjou.

McCarthy was a friend of mine. Whether he went overboard or not, he was of value to his country. A number of liberals think he started the witch-hunt. I think he was witch-hunted himself.
John Wayne.

From what I hear about Communism, I don't like it because it isn't on the level.
Gary Cooper.

The only ism Hollywood believes in is plagiarism.
Dorothy Parker.

As long as I live, I will never be a party to anything as un-American as a blacklist, and any statement purporting to quote me as agreeing to a blacklist is a libel upon me as a good American.
Eric Johnston,
president of the Association of Motion Picture Producers, 1947.

We will not knowingly employ a Communist or a member of any party or group which advocates the overthrow of the Government of the United States by force, or by any illegal or unconstitutional methods.
Statement from the Association of Motion Picture Producers, 24 November 1947.

Of the Unfriendly Ten only two have talent – the other eight are just unfriendly.
Billy Wilder.

They were entombed, most of them, not for being true to themselves, but for sitting up too long with their press releases.
Murray Kempton, on the Hollywood Ten.

Yeah? So where were they when Bugsy Siegel was in trouble?
George Raft,
on being asked to help Hollywood's liberals and left-wingers who were under the threat of blacklisting.

With the crown of thorns I wear, why should I be bothered with a prick like you?
Dorothy Parker,
to a bar-room bore during the period of her blacklisting in the Forties.

It is not enough to have informed – you must also have talent
Sign at Warner Brothers,
where a number of writers found work after having testified against their fellows before the McCarthyite Congressional hearings.

Blacklist, schmacklist – as long as they're all working.
Billy Wilder.

We have many Communists who are splendid writers. They do not have to write Communistically at all, but they have to be watched.
Adolphe Menjou.

Harry was about as much of a Communist as any of the liberals were, which was not much of a Communist at all. He certainly wasn't political – in fact, he was a hell of a snob – but his instincts were all decent, he had loads of friends who were liberal, and he kept them, and he didn't give a damn what your politics were as long as you had talent. But back in those rotten days, which were hysterical with fear, the people who drew up the blacklists never gave a damn for truth. They smeared everyone with their same lousy innuendoes – and that's what happened to Kurnitz.
Anonymous, on the blacklisting of Harry Kurnitz.

During this depression, when the spirit of the people is lower than at any other time, it is a splendid thing that for just fifteen cents an American can go to a movie and look at the smiling face of a baby and forget his troubles.
Franklin Delano Roosevelt, on Shirley Temple, 1935.

I'd rather be right than Roosevelt.
Heywood Broun, mc.1935.

If you don't vote for me, I'll hold by breath.
Anonymous graffito
on posters featuring Shirley Temple when the former child star stood for election in the Sixties.

If it were more than jail, if it were my life, I would give it for what I think democracy is and I don't let cops or judges tell me what I think democracy is.
Dashiell Hammett,
to Lillian Hellman before going to jail for refusing to testify in the Hollywood hearings.

It is not enough to be Hungarian: You have to have talent, too.
Anonymous,
sign at MGM just before World War II.

Our B-17's bombed Budapest last night and destroyed three playwriting factories.
Anonymous,
studio bulletin during World War II.

My status is 8-T- that means I go when the Japs are in the lobby.
George Jessel,
on his draft classification, 1943.

I am not a Jew! I am a citizen of the world! I am not a Communist ! I am a peacemonger!
Charlie Chaplin,
after being attacked in Nazi propaganda.

I'm an American and not a Jew.
David O. Selznick.
to Ben Hecht rejecting one of Hecht's periodic appeals for money for the Zionist cause.

A liberal is a man who leaves the room when the fight starts.
Heywood Broun.

Any reasonable system of taxation should be based on the slogan of 'Soak the rich'.
Heywood Broun.

Babies in silk hats playing with dynamite.
Alexander Woollcott, on diplomats.

I tell you folks, all politics is apple-sauce.
Will Rogers.

To Sam Spiegel, a very brave man. Little does he know that there's a thousand dollars on each of your heads.
Harry Kurnitz,
proposing a toast at a London party hosted by Sam Spiegel and attended only by political exiles from Hollywood:

You've lost all your money and have nothing to lose by not talking. But I made 400,000 dollars last year. I've got to talk.
Elia Kazan,
to Lillian Hellman on their appearances before HUAC.

I think I am leaving by force.
Ring Lardner, Jr.,
after being carried out of the HUAC Hollywood hearings.

There is no lantern by which the crank can be distinguished from the reformer when the night is dark. Just as every conviction begins as a whim so does every emancipator serve his apprenticeship as a crank. A fanatic is a great leader who is just entering the room.
Heywood Broun.

It takes no great perspicacity to detect and to complain of the standardization of American life. So many foreign and domestic commentators have pointed this feature out in exactly the same terms that the comment has become standardized and could be turned out by the thousand on little greeting cards, all from the same type form: 'American life has become too standardized.'
Robert Benchley.

I never vote for anyone. I always vote against.
W. C. Fields.

I don't want to be right: I just want to keep on working.
Arthur Caesar.

I have no further use for America. I wouldn't go back there if Jesus Christ was President.
Charlie Chaplin,
on being forced to leave the United States, 1953.

More men have been elected between sundown and sunup than ever were elected between sunup and sundown.
Will Rogers.

Public opinion in this country runs like a shower bath. We have no temperatures between hot and cold.
Heywood Broun.

They have suffered too much ever to be funny to me.
Charlie Chaplin, on black people.

With the increase in crime during the past decade has come a corresponding increase in crime prevention. Or perhaps it is vice versa.
Robert Benchley.

His mind is so open that the wind whistles through it.
Heywood Broun, on an unnamed news commentator.

No, No! *Jimmy Stewart* for governor – Reagan for his best friend.
Jack L. Warner,
on hearing that former Warner contract player Ronald Reagan was standing for governor of California.

The people of Germany are just as responsible for Hitler as the people of Chicago are for the Chicago 'Tribune'.
Alexander Woollcott,
Last words spoken on the air.

Viewed as drama, the war is somewhat disappointing.
D. W. Griffith, 1918.

We are the first nation in the history of the world to go to the poorhouse in an automobile.
Will Rogers.

All my films have been concerned simply with man as a social animal, although in the 1950s I was a more hopeful person from a liberal standpoint, whereas more recently, in common with many other Americans, I have become somewhat harder in my opinions, presenting possibly a somewhat blacker look at the world today.
Roger Corman, 1970.

Richard Nixon is my President, Ronald Reagan is my Governor, George Murphy is my Senator, Sam Yorty is my Mayor, and the William Morris office is my agent – and you want to know why I'm depressed.
Paul Mazurski, to Larry Tucker.

If I have to lay an egg for my country, I'll do it.
Bob Hope.

I can't understand why some Easterners think it's unusual that California elected Reagan. After all, the state is just going along with the political trend. One of our major industries is motion pictures, so the Governor is an actor. In New York, the nation's financial centre, their Governor is a multi-millionaire financier. In Michigan, the home of the automobile industry, their Governor is a car manufacturer. In Georgia, the state that grows the bulk of our nation's papershell pecans, they elected a nut. I wouldn't be surprised if the next Governor of Florida is a grapefruit.
Groucho Marx and Hal Kantner, 1967.

The great nations have always acted like gangsters, and the small nations like prostitutes.
Stanley Kubrick.

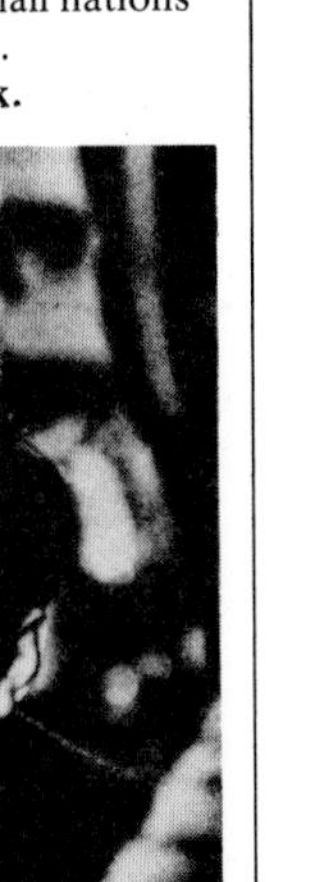

STANLEY KUBRICK.

Chapter 11

Censoring The Dream

LEFT: THE YOUNG BOB HOPE. RIGHT: JEAN RENOIR.

Hollywood buys a good story about a bad girl and has to change it to a bad story about a good girl.
Anonymous, c. 1935.

In a novel a hero can lay ten girls and marry a virgin for a finish. In a movie, this is not allowed. The hero, as well as the heroine, has to be a virgin. The villain can lay anybody he wants, have as much fun as he wants cheating and stealing, getting rich and whipping the servants. But you have to shoot him in the end. When he falls with a bullet in his forehead, it is advisable that he clutch at the Gobelin tapestry on the library wall and bring it down over his head like a symbolic shroud. Also, covered by such a tapestry, the actor does not have to hold his breath while he is being photographed as a dead man.
Herman Mankiewicz, c. 1940.

Any film that isn't fit to be shown to my youngest child, isn't fit to be shown to anybody.
The Chicago Chief of Police, c. 1935.

This industry must have towards that sacred thing, the mind of the child, towards that clean virgin thing, the unmarked slate, the same responsibility, the same care about the impressions made upon it, that the best clergyman or the most inspired teacher of youth would have.
Will Hays.

I have sometimes thought that a part of the value I may have had for the industry was the fact that, despite my long residence in New York, I have somehow remained an unreconstructed Middle Westerner from 'the sticks'.
Will Hays.

No medium has contributed more than the films to the maintenance of the national morale during a period featured by revolutions, riot and political turmoil in other countries. It has been the mission of the screen, without ignoring the serious social problems of the day, to reflect aspiration, achievement, optimism and kindly humour in its entertainment. Historians of the future will not ignore the interesting and significant fact that the movies literally laughed the big bad wolf of depression out of the public.
Will Hays.

The inanities blessed by the Hays Office are more genuinely corrupting than any pornography.
Joseph Wood Krutch.

Will Hays is my shepherd, I shall not want.
He maketh me to lie down in clean postures.
Gene Fowler,
lampooning the Hays Office code.

We are paid to have dirty minds.
John Trevelyan, 1960.

The Americans are nice people but right now they're behaving like small boys who've just discovered what sex is.
John Trevelyan, 1970.

They are doing things on the screen now that I wouldn't do in bed. If I could.
Bob Hope, 1965.

They can't censor the gleam in my eye.
Charles Laughton,
when told he was not allowed to show Edward Moulton-Barretts incestuous relationship in 'The Barretts of Wimpole Street' (1935).

BRITISH BOARD OF FILM CENSORS
133, OXFORD STREET, W.1.
SECRETARY: A. T. L. WATKINS
This is to Certify
that "Yield to the Night"
has been Passed for Public
Exhibition to Adult Audiences
A
E. W. Harris
President

The Hays Office warned us that we couldn't show the heroine as a prostitute. We had to put a sewing machine in her apartment, so in that way she was not a whore but a seamstress.
Fritz Lang,
on shooting 'Man Hunt' (1940).

Yea, though I walk through the alley of the shadow of debt, I will fear no drivel – for the Purity Seal is with me . . .
Gene Fowler.

The producer, director and writer, shackled like a troupe of rheumatic Houdinis, connive, scheme and risk mental hernia to circumvent the censor. Resultant scenes ofttimes are so dizzy that they offend the discerning spectators and drive morons into the park to swing little girls.
Gene Fowler.

Ben Hecht,
asked by Bernie Hyman, head of production at MGM, whether he could come up with 'some gimmick' to keep two lovers out of bed until nearer the end of a particular picture:
Frequently a girl has moral concepts that keep her virtuous until after a trip to the altar. And . . . there are men also who prefer to wait for coitus until after they have married the girl they adore.
Replied Hyman:
Wonderful. We'll try it!

About censorship we feel the way either Mr. Moran or Mr. Mack feels about piccolo playing. 'Even if it's good,' drawls the drawling one, 'I won't like it.'
Franklin Pierce Adams.

Hollywood must never permit censorship to collapse – it's far too good for the box office.
Claude Binyon.

It is in the interest of producers to maintain a certain moral standard since, if they don't do this, the immoral films won't sell.
Jean Renoir.

I don't like it, but nor do I like the absence of it.
Robert Rossen, on censorship.

What critics call dirty in our movies, they call lusty in foreign films.
Billy Wilder.

The cinema needs continual repression of controversy to stave off disaster.
Lord Tyrell, 1936.

The trouble with censors is they worry if a girl has cleavage. They ought to worry if she hasn't any.
Marilyn Monroe.

RIGHT: MARILYN MONROE.

Chapter 12

Comic Cuts

(Buster) Keaton is a distinct asset to the movies. He can attract people who would never think of going to a picture palace to see anything else. Moreover, he can impress a weary world with the vitally important fact that life, after all, is a foolishly inconsequential affair.
Sherwood Anderson.

Laughter comes from children; it's an emotion . . . The great comedians imitate children. That's their ability . . . There is not a great visual comedian that I know of whose every movement is not that of a child. Nothing that Chaplin ever did! Nobody walked as he walked. No grown-up ever went round a corner on one foot. Hardy's action with the tie, Laurel scratching his head, these are the actions of a child. Laurel never cried when he was mad, he never cried when he was hurt, he never cried when he was scared. He only cried when he was confused – that's why it's so funny when he cries.
Hal Roach.

Mack Sennett knew how to do slapstick, but he never knew why he did it. It was instinct with Mack.
Hal Roach.

My Little Chickadee.
Joseph L. Mankiewicz.
Title of W. C. Fields film; the phrase was invented by him as part of a routine he wrote for Fields and Alison Skipworth in 'If I Had a Million', 1932.

The oddest thing about this whole funny business is that the public really wants to laugh, but it's the hardest thing to make them do it. They don't want to cry, yet they will cry at the slightest provocation. Maybe that's why so many comedians want to play tragedy – they want a sort of vacation.
Harry Langdon.

CENTRE: HARRY LANGDON.

Humour is the coward's livery, and there is great wisdom in the popular challenge, 'laugh that off'.
Heywood Broun.

Only things that one could imagine happening to real people, I guess, remain in a person's memory.
Buster Keaton.

The son of a bitch is a ballet dancer! He's the best ballet dancer that ever lived, and if I get a good chance I'll strangle him with my bare hands.
W. C. Fields, on Charlie Chaplin.

Making a joke to shatter reality.
Woody Allen.

The joke of life is the fall of dignity.
Mack Sennett.

He may have been a difficult man, but he had a peculiar sense of what was right – and he stuck by it.
Joseph L. Mankiewicz, on W. C. Fields.

Our comedies are not meant to be laughed at.
The Stern Brothers,
uncles of Carl Laemmle.

Comedy, like sodomy, is an unnatural act.
Marty Feldman.

All I need to make a comedy is a park, a policeman and a pretty girl.
Charlie Chaplin.

I remain just one thing and one thing only, and that is a clown. It places me on a far higher plane than any politician.
Charlie Chaplin, 1960.

I'm a ba-a-a-a-ad boy!
Lou Costello.

MACK SENNETT.

LAUREL AND HARDY.

Martin and Lewis is a very funny fellow.
George S. Kaufman
on the comedy team of Dean Martin and Jerry Lewis.

Everything is funny as long as it is happening to somebody else.
Will Rogers.

A comedian can only last till he either takes himself serious or his audience takes him serious.
Will Rogers.

I have a lesser opinion of comedy . . . A comedy for me has the quality of being a little dessert, a diversion . . . The real meat and potatoes are serious films.
Woody Allen.

In Milwaukee last month a man died laughing over one of his own jokes. That's what makes it so tough for us outsiders. We have to fight home competition.
Robert Benchley.

Je suis Marxiste, tendence Groucho.
Anonymous graffito, Paris, 1968.

It must be difficult, in dealing with so strange a tongue as American, to tell whether an actor is supposed to be funny or not.
Robert Benchley, on the Marx Brothers.

'Cocoanuts' introduced me to the Marx Brothers. 'Cocoanuts' was a comedy; the Marx Brothers are comics; meeting them was a tragedy.
George S. Kaufman.

Satire is something that closes Saturday night.
George S. Kaufman.

Repartee is what you wish you'd said.
Heywood Broun.

I never knew what bicarbonate of soda was until I wrote a Marx Brothers picture.
Herman Mankiewicz.

Humour is grit in the evolutionary process. 'Does it matter?' is the underlying mood in almost every expression of humour. And of course it does matter.
Heywood Broun.

No comic can be great in films without two things – a great story which gives you a character to play, and a great director.
Jack Benny.

Satirists should be heard and not seen.
Sherwood Anderson,
of George Bernard Shaw's screen debut, 1928.

Wit has truth in it; wisecracking is simply calisthenics with words.
Dorothy Parker.

Here's another fine mess you've gotten me into.
Oliver Hardy, to Stan Laurel.

Those two fellows we created, they were nice, very nice people. They never get anywhere because they are both so dumb, but they don't know they're dumb. One of the reasons why people like us, I guess, is because they feel superior to us.
Oliver Hardy.

I lean towards the comedy approach. My whole career has been making films laughing at ourselves (and myself); which is perhaps the reason that all my pictures with one exception ('Lost Horizon') have been about American people. I know Americans better than people of any other country and by knowing them better I think I know what they laugh at and what should be laughed at.
Frank Capra.

All that the comedian has to show for his years of work and aggravation is the echo of forgotten laughter.
Fred Allen.

Lincoln would have loved him.
Carl Sandburg, on comedian Milton Berle.

Chapter 13

The Good, The Bad And The Ugly

LEFT: OTTO PREMINGER. RIGHT: CEDRIC HARDWICKE.

An epic is the easiest kind of picture to make badly.
Charlton Heston.

'Ben Hur'. Loved Ben, hated Hur.
Anonymous capsule review.

Do you have any idea how bad that picture is? I'll tell you. Stay away from the neighbourhood where it's playing – don't even go near that street! It might rain – you could get caught in the downpour, and to keep dry, you'd have to go inside the theatre.
Herman Mankiewicz, on an unnamed film.

Casting is a process whereby a studio decides which of two faces the public is least tired of.
Anonymous.

A double feature is a show that enables you to sit through a picture you don't care to see, so you can see one you don't like.
Henry Morgan.

'I Am a Camera!. Me No Leica.
Anonymous capsule review.

'Aimez-vous Brahms?' Brahms, oui.
Anonymous capsule review.

My most distinguished flop. I've had much less distinguished ones.
Otto Preminger, on 'Saint Joan'.

A great showman who has never bothered to learn anything about making a movie. No one is more skilled at giving the appearance of dealing with large controversial themes in a bold way, without making the tactical error of doing so.
Dwight Macdonald, on Otto Preminger.

Long ago at 20th-Century Fox, I was reading one of the innumerable synopses that were distributed each week and I paused when I came to the name of the hero: Rhett Butler. Undiscouraged, I pressed on. But when I came to the name of the heroine, Scarlett O'Hara, I dropped the whole matter. I had no intention of getting mixed up in another version of Terry and the Pirates and the Dragon Lady and Lace. What fools they were to think they could hoodwink me with rot like that.
Nunnally Johnson.

'Coming Home' is a male supremicist film: men choose between ideas, and women choose between men.
Nancy Dowd.

I would like to recommend this film to those who can stay interested in Ronald Colman's amnesia for two hours and who could with pleasure eat a bowl of Yardley's shaving soap for breakfast.
James Agee, on 'Random Harvest'.

First picture I've ever seen in which the male lead has bigger tits than the female.
Groucho Marx,
asked for his opinion of de Mille's 'Samson and Delilah' which starred Victor Mature and Hedy Lamarr.

No worse than a bad cold.
Harpo Marx,
on the extraordinarily successful play and film 'Abie's Irish Rose'.

The toughest three pictures I ever made.
Joseph L. Mankiewicz, on 'Cleopatra'.

When ten years later I saw the film myself, it was like seeing a corpse in a graveyard.
Eric von Stroheim, on 'Greed'.

You bring me a picture like this and want money for it? You may as well put your hand in my pocket and steal it. It isn't commercial. Everyone in it dies.
Adolph Zukor,
refusing to finance 'Broken Blossoms'.

Maybe a lot of people just didn't want to see Clint Eastwood's leg cut off.
Jennings Lang,
on the relative commercial failure of 'The Beguiled'.

'Samson and Delilah'. A movie for de Millions.
Anonymous capsule review.

Well, we could have the Germans win the war.
Lewis Milestone,
asked if he could give 'All Quiet on the Western Front' a happier ending.

Several tons of dynamite are set off in this picture – none of it under the right people.
James Agee, on 'Tycoon'.

'You Were Meant For Me'. That's what you think.
James Agee, capsule review.

Hedy bit off more than she can chew, so the chewing was done by the rest of the cast, and what was chewed was the scenery.
'Variety'
review of Hedy Lamarr's independent production, 'The Strange Woman'.

HEDY LAMARR.

LEFT: CHARLTON HESTON IN BEN HUR.

Reviewing films is for women and fairies.
Harold Ross.

On Hollywood's theory that the audience knows best, the schoolboy's 'lousy' is the last word in dramatic criticism.
Cedric Hardwicke.

There is a popular misconception to the effect that so-called highbrow critics are prejudiced against red-blooded Western pictures as a matter of principle. All critics are necessarily puny, shrivelled, anaemic old crabs who have never stepped outside the city limits, and therefore know nothing of the ways of clean, two-fisted he-men.
Sherwood Anderson.

I think the picture stinks.
Oscar Levant,
when asked by Darryl Zanuck for an opinion about a new Fox production:
Zanuck:
Who the hell are you to think the picture stinks?
Levant:
Who the hell do you have to be to think the picture stinks?

The picture was so bad they had to do retakes before they could put it on the shelf.
King Vidor.

Ordeal by comment card, known otherwise as death by a thousand cuts.
Cedric Hardwicke,
on the Hollywood sneak preview system.

He hasn't got much to say, but at least he doesn't try to say anything else.
Robert Sherwood, on his own work.

A musical is a series of catastrophes ending with a floor show.
Oscar Levant.

If it were mine, I'd cut it up and sell it for mandolin picks.
Arthur Caesar,
to Darryl Zanuck after a private screening of one of his latest productions.

Like writing history with lightning. And it's all true.
Woodrow Wilson,
on 'The Birth of a Nation'.

A picture with a smile and perhaps a tear.
Opening title of Chaplin's 'The Kid'.

In the first act she becomes a lady. In the second act he becomes a lady.
Alexander Woollcott,
reviewing a play of unparalleled sentimentality.

There are a number of strikingly effective bullfight scenes (in 'Blood and Sand') although it is quite evident that the expensive Signor Valentino is absent from the more strenuous episodes. He is shown making passes at a bull which is only half in the picture. As Will Rogers observes, we shall probably never learn the identity of the hero who held the bull's tail.
Sherwood Anderson.

I will do this film ('Limelight') to the musical score, like a ballet. It is all choreographed in my mind – all that remains is to film it.
Charlie Chaplin.

I made this picture for the Jews of the world.
Charlie Chaplin, on 'The Great Dictator'.

CHARLIE CHAPLIN.

The greatest commercial anticlimax in film history.
Gene Fowler, on 'Intolerance'.

This picture was conceived in a state of emergency, shot in confusion, and wound up in a blind panic.
Joseph L. Mankiewicz,
on his film, the epic and expensive 'Cleopatra' (1962).

Don't be a damn fool, David. This picture is going to be one of the biggest white elephants of all time.
Victor Fleming,
the director, refusing David O. Selznick's offer of a percentage of the profits on 'Gone With The Wind'

One day Ben Schulberg, who ran production (at Paramount), sent a note

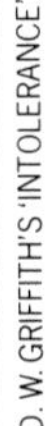
D. W. GRIFFITH'S 'INTOLERANCE'.

around saying that the 1932 Olympic Games were to be held in Los Angeles, and how could we get a story out of that? Well, I went up and talked with him about it, and I said there were only a certain set of plots for athletic pictures – would Jack Oakie carry the ball over the goal line for a touch-down and win Mary Brian, and that sort of thing – and I suggested to Schulberg that he let me do a comedy about the Olympic Games, poke fun at the whole thing, and B.S. went along with it. That's how I got to write 'Million Dollar Legs', which had W.C. Fields and Ben Turpin and a whole batch of comics. Nowadays the art-film students say it was years ahead of its time – that's happened to me a lot since then – but when Paramount released 'Million Dollar Legs' nobody in the U.S. could figure out what the hell it was all about. It wasn't until the picture was sent over to Paris that it became a hit. It ran in one theatre in Paris for two years, and I got a letter from Man Ray, the photographer, telling me how marvellous and surrealistic he'd found the picture to be.

Joseph Mankiewicz.

There is less in this than meets the eye.

Tallulah Bankhead,
after seeing a play by Maeterlinck (also attributed to Robert Benchley after seeing a modernist film).

No matter where you come in during the running, you seem to have missed at least half the picture.

Harry Kurnitz.
on John Huston's film 'Beat the Devil'.

What do they want me to do? Stop now and release it as The Five Commandments.

Cecil B. de Mille,
accused of overspending on 'The Ten Commandments'.

I Aim at the Stars, But Sometimes I Hit London.

Anonymous
comment on the flop film biography of German World War II rocket designer Wernher von Braun, titled 'I Aim At the Stars':

JOE BRA

Chapter 14

Careless Talk

Nothing is as cheap as a hit, no matter how much it cost.
Walter Wanger.

This mug of mine is as plain as a barn door. Why should people pay thirty-five cents to look at it?
Spencer Tracy.

I was a fourteen-year-old boy for thirty years.
Mickey Rooney.

I'm too tired and old and rich for all this, so let's do the scene.
Spencer Tracy,
while working for a modern, 'artistic' director.

You're too little and too fat, but I might give you a job.
D. W. Griffith, to Mary Pickford.

I can't afford to work for only ten thousand dollars a week.
Mary Pickford, to Adolph Zukor.

I have eyes like those of a dead pig.
Marlon Brando.

Not every guy can walk in off the street and be an agent – but *almost* any guy can.
Milton Pickman
(himself a Hollywood agent).

Buddy Hackett, comedian, asked whether he would have paid Liz Taylor the unprecedented fee of one million dollars to play 'Cleopatra': Nah, I'd probably offer her 35,000 dollars . . . and she'd say 'Kiss my ass,' and that's all I want from her anyway.

I'm as pure as the driven slush.
Tallulah Bankhead.

I guess my face is still the same, and so is the dialogue. Only the horses have changed.
Audie Murphy.

Tell her that in America men don't like fat women.
Louis B. Mayer to Greta Garbo's agent.

I am a wife-made man.
Danny Kaye.

If I had the dough, I'd buy up the negative of every film I've ever made, and start one hell of a fire.
Sterling Hayden.

I have a face like the behind of an elephant.
Charles Laughton.

This is for posterity. Everything I do will be on film forever.
Barbra Streisand, on 'Funny Girl'.

Write anything you want about me. Make up something. Hell, I don't care.
Spencer Tracy, to the press.

To a newspaperman a human being is an item with the skin wrapped around it.
Fred Allen.

Some of my best friends are newspaper photographers, and yet I feel that when one or two are gathered together for professional reasons you have a nuisance, and that a dozen or more constitute a plague.
Heywood Broun.

A good listener is not only popular everywhere, but after a while he gets to know something.
Wilson Mizner.

Cecil B. de Mille, much against his will,
Was persuaded to keep Moses, out of the Wars of the Roses.
Anonymous clerihew.

A twenty-one inch prison. I'm delighted with it because it used to be that films were the lowest form of art. Now we've got something to look down on.
Billy Wilder, on television.

I was lucky, you know. I always had a beautiful girl and the money was good. Although I would have done the whole thing over for, oh perhaps, half.
Bob Hope, on his film career.

I like to be introduced as America's foremost actor. It saves the necessity of further effort.
John Barrymore.

Honestly, I think I've stretched a talent which is so thin it's almost transparent over quite an unbelievable term of years.
Bing Crosby.

The Brando school are grabbers, not lovers. If it wasn't that the script says they get the girl, they wouldn't.
Adolphe Menjou.

Let's face it, actors are paid more than they're worth. Producers are idiots for paying what we ask.
James Garner.

Hell, I ain't paid to make good lines sound good. I'm paid to make bad lines sound good.
Walter Huston.

I felt like an impostor, taking all that money for reciting ten or twelve lines of nonsense a day.
Errol Flynn.

I'm only a product like a cake of soap. To be sold as well as possible.
Charles Bronson.

CHARLES BRONSON.

When someone tells you a hardluck story you don't investigate him first – you help him first.
James Cagney.

Dese are de conditions dat prevail.
Jimmy Durante.

That's all there is, there isn't any more.
Ethel Barrymore.

And I'll say of Verlaine too; he was always chasing Rimbauds.
Dorothy Parker, 'The Little Hours'.

A broker is a man who runs your fortune into a shoestring.
Alexander Woollcott.

I can think of forty better places to spend the summer, all of them on Long Island in a hammock.
Harpo Marx,
declining an invitation by Alexander Woollcott to summer on the French Riviera.

To hell with them small towns. I'll take New York.
Jimmy Durante, when asked to play Hamlet.

You can lead a whore to culture, but you can't make her think.
Dorothy Parker,
playing a favourite game of the Algonquin set – 'I Can Give You A Sentence' – with the word 'horticulture'.

It wrecked the art of film for a decade.
Leon Shamroy, on Cinemascope.

The next time I send a dumb sonofabitch to do something, I go myself!
Michael Curtiz.

My forefathers didn't come over on the Mayflower, but they met the boat.
Will Rogers.

The only thing that Jean-Paul Sartre and I have in common is that he over-tips and I over-tip.
Woody Allen.

A mouse studying to be a rat.
Wilson Mizner.

A very simple engineering problem.
Howard Hughes,
on designing a bra for Jane Russell to wear in 'The Outlaw'.

JANE RUSSELL IN 'THE OUTLAW'.

If black people did movies, my premise is that movies would be much shorter, because they wouldn't waste time with a lot of excess shit.
Richard Pryor.

The urban Jewish mentality is being racked with guilt and suffering. . ., feeling one step ahead of trouble and anxiety.
Woody Allen.

I never get so depressed that it interferes with my work. I'm disciplined. I can go into a room every morning and churn it out.
Woody Allen.

Curtiz spoken here.
Anonymous sign at Warner Brothers studio, 1939.

This man Cole Porter, he sticked to purpose of making good music, come hell or hayride.
Mike Curtiz,
on his Porter biopic 'Night and Day'.

An agent is a guy who is sore because the actor gets 90% of what he makes.
Alva Johnston.

Congratulations on getting the other ninety percent.
Telegram to agent Leland Hayward
on the occasion of his marriage to his client, Margaret Sullavan.

A man has one hundred dollars and you leave him with two – that's subtraction.
Mae West.

There are certain things in life you just can't sacrifice.
Clint Eastwood, on beer.

There was I trapped. Trapped like a trap in a trap.
Dorothy Parker.

Very simple, they had to have someone to listen.
Harpo Marx,
asked how he survived the rarified atmosphere of wit that pervaded the Thanatopsis poker club upstairs at the famed Algonquin Hotel.

In case of an air-raid, go directly to RKO – they haven't had a hit in years.
Anonymous, 1942.

Brevity is the soul of lingerie, as the petticoat said to the chemise.
Dorothy Parker.
A caption by her written during her short career at Vogue magazine.

Military intelligence is a contradiction in terms.
Groucho Marx.

There is a natural hootchy-kootchy to a goldfish.
Walt Disney.

Television is a medium – so called because it is neither rare nor well done.
Ernie Kovacs.

They're lucky if they don't stay in it long and if they don't learn.
George Cukor,
on television as an actors' training-ground.

Why should people go out and pay money to see bad films when they can stay at home and see bad television for nothing.
Sam Goldwyn, 1956.

Television is chewing gum for the eyes.
Frank Lloyd Wright.

The bland leading the bland.
Anonymous comment on television.

Salary is no object; I want only enough to keep body and soul apart.
Dorothy Parker, discussing a job offer.

My kids never had the advantage I had. I was born poor.
Kirk Douglas.

Pharaoh (looking at the infant Moses in his daughter's arms): My God! What an ugly kid! Where did you get *him?* Pharaoh's daughter: I can't understand it. He looked so good in the rushes.
Hollywood joke of the de Mille era.

How do you think a smash hit would go today?
Harry Ruby, to a producer.

Men don't like nobility in women. Not any men. I suppose it is because the men like to have the copyrights on nobility – if there is going to be anything like that in a relationship.
Dorothy Parker.

From now on we're going to have to call up our agent every hour and give him the time.
Nat Perrin,
after he and Arthur Sheekman had received two watches as payment for a small service they had done for a studio.

I'll go on shooting the bastards until they learn to shit green.
W. C. Fields,
after being told off by a neighbour for taking pot-shots at the birds on the lawn of his Beverly Hills home.

The test of a first-rate intelligence is the ability to hold two opposed ideas in the mind at the same time and still retain the ability to function.
F. Scott Fitzgerald, 'The Crack-Up'.

Higgledy piggledy, my white hen;
She lays eggs for gentlemen.
You cannot persuade her with gun or lariat
To come across for the proletariat.
Dorothy Parker.
Impromptu verse written for Somerset Maugham.

All I know is just what I read in the papers.
Will Rogers.

With Cinemascope, the director is at last free of the camera and has an unparalleled chance to demonstrate his ability to move actors logically and dramatically . . . Cinemascope places a director somewhere between the stage and the screen technique.
Henry Koster.

There was a time when all I looked for was a good story, but nowadays everything has to look the size of Mount Rushmore, and the actors in close-up look as though they belong there.
Fritz Lang, on Cinemascope.

The worst shape ever devised.
Rouben Mamoulian, on Cinemascope.

It's fine if you want a system that shows a boa constrictor to better advantage than a man.
George Stevens, on Cinemascope.

A wide screen makes a bad film twice as bad.
Sam Goldwyn.

It is a formula for a funeral, or for snakes, but not for human beings.
Fritz Lang, on Cinemascope.

Why not keep the screen the same size and reduce the size of the audience?
Irving Brecher, on Cinemascope.

I don't care to belong to any social organisation that will accept me as a member.
Groucho Marx,
refusing an invitation to join a Hollywood club.

A nine-days wonder, and I came in on the ninth day.
Alfred Hitchcock, on 3-D.

Chapter 15

Inserts

Treat a whore like a lady and a lady like a whore.
Wilson Mizner.

His voice was intimate as the rustle of sheets, and he kissed easily.
Dorothy Parker,
'Dusk Before Fireworks'.

Bing, I'd roll in the hay with her if she was a real rabbi.
Barney Dean,
Jewish gag-writer, on the set of 'The Bells of St. Mary's, when asked by Bing Crosby if he could 'roll in the hay' with Ingrid Bergman if she were a real nun:

Like everyone else's my sex-life went in circles. Sometimes I was potent, other times disappointing.
Charlie Chaplin.

When a woman appealed to him, Bogart waited for her like the flame waits for the moth.
Louise Brooks.

Edna Ferber,
who often worked with George S. Kaufman in her Algonquin suite, to a desk clerk, who inquired 'Is there a gentleman in your room?':
Wait a minute and I'll ask him.

A sex symbol becomes a thing. I hate being a thing.
Marilyn Monroe.

A hard man is good to find.
Mae West.

Baby, I went to night school.
Mae West,
asked how she knew so much about men.

It isn't what I do, but how I do it. It isn't what I say, but how I say it. And how I look when I do it and say it.
Mae West.

Scratch a lover, and find a foe.
Dorothy Parker.

Sex appeal is fifty percent what you've got and fifty percent what people think you've got.
Attributed to Sophia Loren.

It's not the men in my life, it's the life in my men that counts.
Mae West.

When I'm good I'm very good, but when I'm bad I'm better.
Mae West.

Let's forget about the six feet and talk about the seven inches.
Mae West,
on being told by a tall young man that he was six feet seven inches.

Whenever I'm caught between two evils, I take the one I've never tried.
Mae West.

Certainly most movie executives were making love to the starlets. But then, so were most of us actors.
Richard Burton.

I may not be a great actress but I've become the greatest at screen orgasms. Ten seconds of heavy breathing, roll your head from side to side, simulate a slight asthma attack and die a little.
Candice Bergen.

A nude girl is a nude girl and that's that; and there's no way you can make a star out of a nude girl.
Frank Capra, 1972.

The difference with my leading ladies is that they're usually a little more svelte. They don't have their sex hanging around them like baubles.
Alfred Hitchcock.

Women are like elephants to me. I like to look at them, but I wouldn't want to own one.
W.C. Fields.

One cubic foot less of space and it would have constituted adultery.
Robert Benchley,
commenting on the small office he had once shared with Dorothy Parker.

Any girl can be glamorous. All you have to do is stand still and look stupid.
Hedy Lamarr.

RICHARD BURTON.

If all those sweet young things present were laid end to end, I wouldn't be at all surprised.
Dorothy Parker,
commenting on a Yale prom (also said to refer to Hollywood starlets).

Being a sex symbol is a heavy load to carry, especially when one is tired, hurt and bewildered.
Clara Bow.

Just as a Hollywood pin-up represents sex to dissatisfied erotics, so I represented the ideal daughter millions of fathers and mothers wished they had.
Deanna Durbin.

DEANNA DURBIN.

There are various forms of a certain disease, the victim of which is unable to say 'No.' Some of these forms are more serious than others and often lead to electrocution or marriage.
Robert Benchley.

To me love for a person is respect for individual feelings – respecting privacy and accepting faults.
Clint Eastwood.

I have no advice to give to young actors. To young, struggling actresses my advice is to keep struggling. If you struggle long enough, you will never get into trouble and if you never get into trouble, you will never be much of an actress.
Groucho Marx.

Pretty near any complaint you make about wives, when it is true they will probably resent it. But I often ask myself the question could I get along without them? And the answer to that is that I got along without none for twenty-five years and never felt better in my life.
Ring Lardner.

The only real argument for marriage is that it remains the best method for getting acquainted.
Heywood Broun.

If I found a man who had 15 million dollars, would sign over half of it to me before the marriage, and guarantee he'd be dead within a year.
Bette Davis,
asked whether she would consider marrying for a fifth time.

I'm not a real movie star – I still got the same wife I started out with twenty eight years ago.
Will Rogers.

It's a matter of compatibility. We both love to fight.
Harry Tugend,
asked why his marriage had lasted forty years.

Barbara Stanwyck is my favourite. My God, I could just sit and dream of being married to her, having a little cottage out in the hills, vines around the door. I'd come home from the office, tired, weary, and I'd be met by Barbara, walking through the door holding an apple pie that she had cooked herself. And wearing no drawers.
Herman Mankiewicz.

There will be sex after death – we just won't be able to feel it.
Lily Tomlin.

In Hollywood all marriages are happy. It's trying to live together afterwards that causes the problems.
Shelley Winters.

You'll never know how dull this town is until you move here with your wife and kids.
Martin Ragaway.

Now she's kosher, he can eat her.
Oscar Levant,
on Marilyn Monroe's marriage to Jewish playwright Arthur Miller (Monroe had undergone instruction in Judaism.)

Where's the man could ease a heart
Like a satin gown?
Dorothy Parker, 'The Satin Dress'.

I never loved another person the way I love myself.
Mae West.

God, for two people to be able to live together for the rest of their lives is almost unnatural.
Jane Fonda.

She sleeps alone at last.
Robert Benchley,
suggesting an epitaph for an unnamed movie queen whose love-life had been notorious.

Most good women are hidden treasures who are only safe because nobody looks for them.
Dorothy Parker.

I've been around so long, I knew Doris Day before she was a virgin.
Groucho Marx,
also attributed to Oscar Levant.

Is that a pistol in your pocket, or are you just pleased to see me?
Mae West.

All I need is room enough to lay a hat and a few friends.
Dorothy Parker,
while looking for a new apartment.

One night at a flossy party Don appeared on the dance floor in a long overcoat. 'That's silly and showing off, to dance in an overcoat,' said the great lady of films in his arms. 'Please take it off.' Don did. He had nothing on underneath.
Ben Hecht,
on humorous writer Donald Ogden Stewart.

I don't want to see any faces at this party that I haven't sat on.
Unnamed Hollywood actress.

Location shooting is the Rites of Spring for certain members of the crew, who may even be happily married, and for young cast members who have never been away from home before. Holiday Inns across America are probably host to more sprung beds and screaming orgasms when a movie company comes to town than at any other time.
Steven Spielberg.

I remember Harry Tugend's wonderful crack about a certain film star, during World War II, when Tugend was trying to be a producer and hating it. He said. 'You know, this is a lousy job. You got to sit and talk to that bird brain seriously about whether or not this part is going to be good for her career and at the same time you got to keep from being raped.' Whereat a rather innocent young man piped up, 'You mean to say she's a nymphomaniac?' Harry frowned off into the distance and sighed and said slowly, 'Well, I guess she would be, if they could get her quieted down a little.'
Raymond Chandler.

Men seldom make passes
At girls who wear glasses.
Dorothy Parker.

Dorothy Parker,
at a party where the guests played a game of 'ducking for apples'
There, but for a typographical error, is the story of my life.

To put it bluntly, I seem to be a whole superstructure with no foundation. But I'm working on the foundation.
Marilyn Monroe.

Egghead weds hourglass
Newspaper headline
announcing Arthur Miller and Marily Monroe's marriage.

Marilyn Monroe,
when asked what she wore to bed.
Chanel No. 5.

Marilyn Monroe,
when asked by a reporter if she 'had anything on' in bed.

Sex is part of nature, and I go along with nature.
Marilyn Monroe.

Any of my indiscretions were with people, not actresses.
Darryl F. Zanuck.

The ability to make love frivolously is the chief characteristic which distinguishes human beings from the beasts.
Heywood Broun.

When you get a sex story in biblical garb, you can open your own mint.
Darryl F. Zanuck.

In Hollywood, the eternal triangle consists of an actor, his wife and himself.
Anonymous.

A girl's best friend is her mutter.
Dorothy Parker.

Women won't let me stay single, and I won't let myself stay married.
Errol Flynn.

Chapter 16

Life And Life Only

LEFT: CARY GRANT. RIGHT: RUDOLPH VALENTINO.

I have a child and I've made a few people happy. That is all.
Marlene Dietrich.

I've always found insects exciting.
Luis Bunuel.

Everyone tells me I've had such an interesting life, but sometimes I think it's been nothing but stomach disturbances and self-concern.
Cary Grant.

My involvement goes deeper than acting or directing. I love every aspect of the creation of motion pictures and I guess I am committed to it for life.
Clint Eastwood.

There were times when my pants were so thin I could sit on a dime and know if it was heads or tails.
Spencer Tracy.

A man should control his life. Mine is controlling me.
Rudolph Valentino, 1926.

I may not have come up the hard way, but I've come up the whole way.
Bryan Forbes.

They have all four seasons in one day.
Woody Allen,
on why he likes London.

Unable obtain bidet. Suggest handstand in shower.
Billy Wilder in Paris.
Telegram to his wife who had asked him to buy a bidet.

Nothing is more responsible for the good old days than a bad memory.
Franklin Pierce Adams.

Look at me: I worked my way up from nothing to a state of extreme poverty.
Groucho Marx, in 'Monkey Business'.

France is a country where the money falls apart in your hands and you can't tear the toilet paper.
Billy Wilder.

I never want to get used to anything I may someday have to do without.
Fred Allen,
explaining his legendary parsimony.

The less I behave like Whistler's Mother the night before, the more I look like her the morning after.
Tallulah Bankhead,
after having celebrated rather too much at one of Dorothy Parker's parties (Whistler's Mother was Parker's name for Bankhead).

The way to a man's mouth is through his stomach.
Robert Benchley.

People don't know my real self and they're not about to find out.
Yul Brynner.

LEFT: YUL BRYNNER.

From birth to age eighteen, a girl needs good parents. From eighteen to thirty-five, she needs good looks. From thirty-five to fifty-five, she needs a good personality. From fifty-five on, she needs good cash.
Sophie Tucker.

Wherever you go, especially if you're in a strange town, you must always find yourself a good whorehouse to stay at – they always serve the best breakfasts. After all, when a staff has been working all night, it stands to reason they'll be very hungry.
Arthur Caesar.

You have to believe in yourself, that's the secret.
Charlie Chaplin.

One man's Mede is another man's Persian.
George S. Kaufman.

I fold my tens like the Arabs, and as silently steal away.
George S. Kaufman,
after collecting his winnings at a Thanatopsis Club poker session.

I went through it once but it was closed.
George S. Kaufman,
on Boston (also attributed to W. C. Fields on Philadelphia).

She put her heart before the course.
George S. Kaufman,
on being told that one of his daughter's fellow students had eloped.

Frenchmen drink wine like we used to drink water before Prohibition.
Ring Lardner.

I never heard of a good debt.
Ring Lardner.

God is going to have to answer to His maker for this part of the country.
Harry Ruby,
after a tour of Texas army bases with Groucho Marx.

I've been in 'Who's Who' and I know what's what, but this is the first time I've ever been in a dictionary.
Mae West,
on hearing that a life jacket had been named after her.

When we talk about the computer governed society, the establishment, and I say why don't you like it, why do you despise it? – the answer is always, 'Because it has no heart'.
Fritz Lang.

I don't think any good will come out of modern technology as it is used in the United States today.
Fritz Lang, 1978.

A very self-sufficient human being is becoming an almost mythical character in our day and age.
Clint Eastwood.

What is success? It is a toy balloon among children armed with pins.
Gene Fowler.

Always be pleasant to the people you meet on the way up. They are always the people you meet on the way down.
Wilson Mizner
(also attributed to Jimmy Durante).

You've got to love something enough to kill it.
Martin Scorsese.

Loneliness is repellent. It has a subtle aura of sadness, an inadequacy to attract or interest. One feels slightly ashamed of it. But, to a degree, it is the theme of everyone.
Charlie Chaplin.

Civilisation is only skin deep and I'm afraid man is basically evil.
Ralph Nelson.

I believe in the complete innocence of children. They have no idea of good and evil. It's an acquired taste.
Sam Peckinpah.

It's unhealthy when your whole life comes back to you in a nostalgic way. You're trapped into the fallacy of irony having meaning. You think these things mean something when they don't.
Woody Allen.

Life's a tough proposition, and the first hundred years are the hardest.
Wilson Mizner.

So little time, so little to do.
Oscar Levant.

Four be the things I am wiser to know:
Idleness, sorrow, a friend and a foe.
Four be the things I'd be better without:
Love, curiosity, freckles and doubt.
Dorothy Parker, 'Inventory'.

You get a new chimpanzee and put him in Griffith Park Zoo and everybody rushes to look him over. And if the keepers don't feed him well and take the best care of him, the public raises hell. But you put a person in a cage and nobody seems to care how he gets along. And it doesn't even amuse the children.
Robert Mitchum,
after being jailed on a marijuana charge, 1948.

Sorrow is tranquility remembered in emotion.
Dorothy Parker.

The man who has cured himself of B.O. and halitosis, has learned French to surprise the waiter, and the saxophone to amuse the company, may find that people still avoid him because they do not like him.
Heywood Broun.

DIANE KEATON.

Life is nothing but a series of conflicts, in a way, surmounting one and coming to another.
Diane Keaton.

In the march up to the heights of fame there comes a spot close to the summit in which a man reads 'nothing but detective stories'.
Heywood Broun.

It's like a bank. Lots of doors, plenty of tellers – but only one that can okay the cheque.
Arthur Caesar, on religion.

I have God, and when you get to know Him, you find He's a livin' doll.
Jane Russell.

At a very early age I was frightened by a policeman. I'd been a bad boy. I can't remember what I'd done, but my father sent me to the police station with a note. The policeman read the note and locked me in a cell – for five minutes . . . I've been trying to escape from that cell ever since.
Alfred Hitchcock.

We are not punished for our sins, but by them.
Arthur Caesar.

There is no religious feeling that can make any thinking person happy.
Woody Allen.

Life is a concentration camp. You're stuck here and there's no way out, and you can only rage impotently against your persecutors.
Woody Allen.

It is in the thirties that we want friends. In the forties we know that they won't save us any more than love did.
F. Scott Fitzgerald.

I can't seem to bring myself to say, 'Well, I guess I'll be toddling along.' It isn't that I can't toddle. It's that I can't guess I'll toddle.
Robert Benchley,
an inveterate party-goer, on his evident inability to leave company.

Obscenity is such a tiny kingdom that a single tour covers it completely.
Heywood Broun.

Life is a copycat and can be bullied into following the master artist who bids it come to heel.
Heywood Broun.

It is not fair that I should thwart and crush great eagerness for existence for the sake of the extremely mild diversion I get from fishing. They told me that the fish cared very little and that they were cold-blooded and felt no pain. But they were not fish who told me.
Heywood Broun.

Tell us your phobias and we will tell you what you are afraid of.
Robert Benchley.

A dog teaches a boy fidelity, perseverance, and to turn around three times before lying down.
Robert Benchley.

If we can develop some way in which a man can doze in public and still keep from making a monkey of himself, we have removed one of the big obstacles to human happiness in modern civilization.
Robert Benchley.

In America there are two classes of travel – first class and with children.
Robert Benchley.

You can't teach an old dogma new tricks.
Dorothy Parker.

Merely as an observer of natural phenomena I am fascinated by my own personal appearance. This doesn't mean that I am *pleased* with it, mind you, or that I can even tolerate it. I simply have a morbid interest in it.
Robert Benchley.

Everyone in the world is Christ and they are all crucified.
Sherwood Anderson.

If at first you don't succeed, try again. Then quit – no use being a damn fool about it.
W. C. Fields.

Woman's life must be wrapped up in a man, and the cleverest woman on earth is the biggest fool with a man.
Dorothy Parker.

Anyone who hates small dogs and children can't be all bad.
W. C. Fields.
(variously quoted as 'animals and children' or just 'children'.)

Anyone who tells you he has invented something new is a fool or a liar or both.
Mack Sennett.

Disneyland – the biggest people trap ever built by a mouse.
Anonymous.

Wilson Mizner, a gambler, wit, and playwright, was brought into a courtroom on some charge or other. During the proceedings, the judge said angrily, 'Are you trying to show contempt of court?' To which Mizner replied, 'No, Your Honour, I am trying to conceal it.'
Irving Wallace.

But I, despite expert advice
keep doing things I think are nice
and though to good I never come –
Inseparable my nose and thumb.
Dorothy Parker.

I suffer from what used to be called Sir tax. A knighthood inflates the cost of living beyond belief.
Cedric Hardwicke.

'F.E.B.F.' (Fuck Everyone But Fields')
W. C. Fields's
only 'charity'

Is it, perhaps, a blessing of the Divine Projectionist that the reels nearest 'The End' move more swiftly? Is He gently reminding us that the work we have left must be our best work, for there is no time for anything less than our best?
Cecil B. de Mille.

My false poetic dream has always been to meet a female bank teller from Kansas, with hay in her hair, and go off and marry and live on a dairy farm in Wisconsin. Of course, that's the last thing I'd ever want to do . . . If I were given my secret wish to live a rural life in the Mid West, I'd be the unhappiest boy on the farm.
Steven Spielberg.

Every radish I ever pulled up seemed to have a mortgage attached to it.
Ed Wynn, on why he sold his farm.

FROM LEFT TO RIGHT: JOSE FERRER, KEENAN WYNN AND FATHER ED WYNN.

Chapter 17

Drink... And Other Exits

LEFT: W.C. FIELDS. RIGHT: THE YOUNG FRANK SINATRA

Don't worry, Arthur – the white wine came up with the fish.
Herman Mankiewicz,
to producer Arthur Hornblow, Jr., after being sick at one of Hornblow's exclusive parties.

(Elizabeth Taylor and Richard Burton) offered me a drink and rolled a liquor cart in from their bedroom which was its permanent abode, and the conversation afterwards was limited to a discussion of 17th century poetry.
William Fadiman.

My father once told me that if you are cold sober and haven't had a drink in weeks and five sane and intelligent people look at you and tell you you are dead drunk, the best thing to do is not to argue but lie down and take a nap for an hour.
Joseph Schenck.

I must have a drink of breakfast.
W. C. Fields.

I never drink water – fish fuck in it!
W. C. Fields.

I exercise extreme self-control. I never drink anything stronger than gin before breakfast.
W. C. Fields.

Somebody left the cork out of my lunch.
W. C. Fields.

Cocaine isn't habit-forming. I should know – I've been using it for years.
Tallulah Bankhead.

Three highballs and I think I'm St. Francis of Assisi.
Dorothy Parker.

So who's in a hurry?
Robert Benchley,
on being told that his favourite drink was 'slow-poison'.

Let's get out of these wet clothes and into a dry martini.
Robert Benchley.
(also attributed to Alexander Woollcott).

Any port in a storm.
Heywood Broun,
after drinking 'a certain inferior liquor'.

I got Mark Hellinger so drunk last night that it took three bellboys to put me to bed.
W. C. Fields.
(Hellinger's capacity for alcohol was the object of wonder, even for an imbiber of Fields' legendary stature).

Doctors want to keep you alive. I want to *live*,
Alexander Woollcott.
shortly before his death.

I don't trust any bastard who doesn't drink.
Humphrey Bogart.

Harry Cohn,
cabling director Lewis Milestone whose filming schedule for 'The Captain Hates the Sea' was being seriously disrupted by the drinking habits of such notorious drunks as John Gilbert, Walter Connelly, Victor McLaglen, Walter Catlett and Leon Errol:
Hurry up, the cost is staggering.
Milestone's return cable:
So is the Cast.

You know you've had a few too many when you come home and find cold scrambled eggs on top of last night's lamb chops.
Ring Lardner.

She thinks she doesn't get old. She told me once it was her cameraman who was getting older. She wanted me to fire him.
Joe Pasternak, on Doris Day.

Did you ever catch George Jessel at a funeral? It's wonderful. All through the years he makes notes on his friends. He wants to be ready.
Eddie Cantor.

He's the kind of guy that, when he dies, he's going up to heaven and give God a bad time for making him bald.
Marlon Brando, on Frank Sinatra.

When I die, be sure the services are in the morning, so my friends can get to the track and not lose any time they need for betting.
Arthur Caesar.

Guns aren't lawful;
Nooses give;
Gas smells awful;
You might as well live.
Dorothy Parker, 'Résumé'.

Three men sit down to a bottle of brandy and divide it equally between them. When they have finished the bottle one of them leaves the room, and the other two try to guess who left.
Alexander Woollcott.

Enjoyed it! One more drink and I'd have been under the host.
Dorothy Parker,
asked if she had enjoyed a cocktail party.

Marshall Neilan ruined himself with liquor and indifference and bitterness. He became a humorous cynic. But liquor did it.
Allan Dwan.

I was in love with a beautiful blonde once, she drove me to drink. 'Tis the one thing I'm indebted to her for.
W. C. Fields.

If I had any decency, I'd be dead. Most of my friends are.
Dorothy Parker,
on her seventieth birthday, 1963.

Old age is the only disease you don't look forward to being cured of:
Everett Sloane, in 'Citizen Kane'.

The hell with the hair on your head. It's the hair on your chest that counts.
Humphrey Bogart, on growing old.

Being an old maid is like death by drowning, a really delightful sensation after you cease to struggle.
Edna Ferber.

I look wonderful for a *woman* my age, but not for a man. I was downtown last week and saw a building as old as I am. It looked terrible.
Ed Wynn,
on being told how good he looked for a man approaching 80.

Retirement at 65 is ridiculous. When I was 65 I still had pimples.
George Burns.

GEORGE BURNS AND GRACIE ALLEN

When I die, just skin me out and put me up on old Trigger and I'll be happy.
Roy Rogers.

One day I shall probably talk myself to death. Those who live by the word shall perish by the word.
Alexander Woollcott.

I don't want to achieve immortality through my work. I want to achieve it through not dying.
Woody Allen.

He was an average guy who could carry a tune.
Bing Crosby,
self-composed epitaph.

On the whole, I'd rather be in Philadelphia.
W. C. Fields,
self-composed epitaph.

He was lucky – and he knew it.
Cary Grant,
self-composed epitaph.

A nice part – only four 'sides', but good company and in for a long run.
Edward Everett Horton,
self-composed epitaph.

Well, I've played everything but a harp.
Lionel Barrymore,
self-composed epitaph.

This is too deep for me.
Hedy Lamarr,
self-composed epitaph.

All the things I really like to do are either immoral, illegal or fattening.
Alexander Woollcott.

Did you hear about my operation?
Warner Baxter,
self-composed epitaph.

Here's something I want to get off my chest.
William Haines,
self-composed epitaph.

A gentleman farmer goes back to the soil.
Lewis Stone,
self-composed epitaph.

Do not disturb.
Constance Bennett,
self-composed epitaph.

At last I get top-billing.
Wallace Ford,
self-composed epitaph.

Now I've laid me down to die
I pray my neighbours not to pry
Too deeply into sins that I
Not only cannot here deny
But much enjoyed – as time flew by.
Preston Sturges,
self-composed epitaph.

I was very ill last summer. For a while, I thought I was a goner. I woke up one night in my hospital bed, and I saw, standing there, a tall man, wearing a white robe, with a long white beard. I said, 'Who are you?' He said, 'I am the Holy Ghost.' I said, 'Where are the Father and the Son?' He said, 'They're out of town.' I'm not a religious man, but it's things like this that make you stop and think.
Harry Ruby.

ROY ROGERS.

What the hell. It's a better line than 'Services will be private'.
Jack Warner,
commenting on a newspaper article which described him, in 1970, as 'nearing eighty'.

With my luck, I'll get a wooden leg from a tree with 'John Loves Mary' carved on it.
Arthur Caesar, on his amputation.

Die? I should say not, old fellow. No Barrymore would allow such a conventional thing to happen to him.
John Barrymore,
during his final illness.

Why should I talk to you, I've just been talking to your boss.
Wilson Mizner,
on his death-bed to a priest.

You understand that last night was only a comedy.
Paul Bern,
in his cryptic suicide note to his wife, Jean Harlow.

Excuse my dust.
This is on me.
Dorothy Parker.
Epitaphs for herself.

Over my dead body.
George S. Kaufman,
suggesting his own epitaph.

Chapter 18

Gone With The Wind

LEFT: VINCENT PRICE. RIGHT: ROUBEN MAMOULIAN.

The movies languish as a fine art because the men who determine what is to get into them haven't the slightest visible notion that such a thing as a fine art exists.
H. L. Mencken, 1927.

Hollywood might have become the centre of a new human expression if it hadn't been grabbed by a little group of book-keepers.
David O. Selznick.

Some say, 'What is the salvation of the movies?' I say run 'em backwards. It can't hurt 'em and it's worth a trial.
Will Rogers.

Let's show the movies in the street – and drive the people back into the theatres.
Nunnally Johnson,
at a Universal International crisis meeting in the fifties.

There's nothing wrong with this business that a star worth 10,000 dollars a week can't cure.
Nicholas Schenck.

There's nothing wrong with the picture business that a good picture can't cure.
Nicholas Schenck.

The surest sign of depression in the industry is not the cutting-down of stars' salaries or the dropping of contract players or the reductions of work crews. The surest sign is when a major studio begins laying off relatives.
Irvin S. Cobb.

In the wave of economy that studios generally have when they get desperate, they drop a few hundred-dollar-a-week employees and then hire a four-thousand-a-week executive.
Joseph M. Schenck.

There's still a lot of the same old kind of thinking around . . . The only thing the studios have to offer a young film-maker these days is their distribution machinery.
Dennis Hopper, 1970.

The end of Hollywood was always predictable. There were always financial crises. Someone would come out from the East and announce that the business was in deep trouble, and, literally, what would happen was that they'd reduce the number of matzo balls in Louie Mayer's chicken soup at the commissary from three to two in each portion. Then they'd fire a couple of secretaries and feel virtuous.
Joseph L. Mankiewicz.

As an American I want to see American pictures succeed, and I believe very strongly in the future of the motion picture. As board chairman of Gulf & Western, I oversee all our divisions. One of them is called Leisure Time, and Paramount is just a part of it. We also operate cable TV companies, music companies, recording companies – in Canada the largest theatre chain in North America . . . There is a tremendous future in the leisure field. The revolution in the industry is creating unparalleled opportunities for those who want to learn the lessons of the past. From this shake-out in Hollywood will come something sound and firm.
Charles G. Bluhdorn, 1970.

It's easy enough to make fun of a film distributor today, but how can you help but feel sorry for the poor bastard? He's faced with the daily decision whether or not to commit large sums of capital to producers who want to make pictures for release a year from now. Now we all realise that exhibitors don't have a clue about what the kids want to see today. How can anyone possibly know what kids will want to see a year from now?
Arthur Mayer.

In the old days you could make a film for £100,000 and get your money back from people sheltering from the rain.
Michael Winner.

In the old days you called the actor and made a deal with him. Now, they bring an army.
Jack Warner.

In the old days we had the time and money to give prospective stars a slow build-up. Today, an actor makes it fast or he doesn't make it at all.
Hal Wallis.

In the old days, villains had moustaches and kicked the dog. Audiences are smarter today. They don't want their villain to be thrown at them with green limelight on his face. They want an ordinary human being with failings.
Alfred Hitchcock.

We have forsaken the magic of the cinema. We have gotten too far away from the cinematic effects achievable by camera angles and creative editing.
Rouben Mamoulian, 1957.

Hollywood film-making of today is stooping to cheap salacious pornography in a crazy bastardization of a great art.
Frank Capra.

Oh – when it closes.
Eleanor Lewis,
as a small girl recently moved to Hollywood, asked when she would be leaving.

My boy, *these* are the good old days.
Jack L. Warner,
at a lavish Hollywood party in the fifties.

Working at Paramount in the 30s was absolutely marvellous. You just walked across the lot and there they were: von Sternberg, Dietrich, Gary Cooper, Leo McCarey, Lubitsch. We made pictures then. Today we spend 80 per cent of the time making deals and 20 per cent making pictures.
Billy Wilder.

The number of paid film admissions in the United States this year will be the lowest in the history of the movie business since the advent of sound.
Gordon Stulberg, 1971.

Stupidity got us into this mess – why can't it get us out?
Will Rogers.

FRANK CAPRA.

One of the deaths of Hollywood is that they tried to make everyone look normal. Some of the actresses who are around today look and sound like my niece in Scarsdale. I love my niece in Scarsdale, but I wouldn't pay to see her act.
Vincent Price.

I predict that within five years you will be able to make a ten million dollar film and get all your money back in one night. There will be 25 million homes with cable TV or cassettes.
Joseph Levine, 1970.

Suddenly, the whole face and temper of our town has changed. The laughter is a little uneasy, the humour has turned black, and we are in the grip of a change like no other we have witnessed before . . . The giants have gone and in their place we have the dodgers. Our town is facing the bleakest year in recent memory. The town itself, the collection of artists and craftsmen who have made Hollywood unique in the world, is slowly breaking up. And no-one is really doing anything about it.
Melville Shavelson, 1971.

Experience has long since prepared us to accept the uncomfortable fact that the best work in motion pictures – the most intelligent, progressive, astute, and alert to what is happening to people – is being done abroad.
Bosley Crowthers.

They break the rules – often without knowing the rules are there, which is funny.
Dalton Trumbo,
on the Hollywood 'new wave'.

You've got to gamble. The movie industry isn't a slide rule business and never will be. It's still the world's biggest crap game.
Richard Zanuck.

Most movies these days are made for nobody; the proportion of movies that fail commercially is at an all-time high, and now when they fail they often fail mercilessly – sometimes on the opening day of a first-run movie a theatre does not sell a single ticket – so that investing money in movies is becoming a fantastic long-shot gamble against public apathy.
Pauline Kael, 1972.

There were giants in the industry. Now it is an era of midgets and conglomerates.
Otto Preminger.

Chapter 19

In Living Memory

LEFT: GRETA GARBO. RIGHT: EDWARD G. ROBINSON.

You ain't heard nothing yet.
Al Jolson,
in 'The Jazz Singer', the first commercially successful synchronised sound movie.

Tennis, anyone?
Humphrey Bogart,
the first line he spoke on the professional stage.

Reach for the sky!
Tom Mix.

I never said, 'I want to be alone'. I only said, 'I want to be let alone'.
Greta Garbo.

I want to be alone.
Greta Garbo, in 'Grand Hotel'.

Never give a sucker an even break.
Edward Francis Albee
(also attributed to W. C. Fields).

Bury my heart at Wounded Knee.
Stephen Vincent Benét, 1927.

Compliment to Mae West in 'Night After Night': 'Goodness, what beautiful diamonds,'
Mae West:
'Goodness had nothing to do with it, dearie'.

I've been things and seen places.
Mae West,
in 'She Done Him Wrong'.

Play It Again, Sam.
Title of stage play and film written by
Woody Allen.

You Can't Take It With You.
George S. Kaufman, title of play and film.

Me Tarzan, you Jane.
Johnny Weissmuller,
in 'Tarzan the Ape Man'.

Gentlemen Prefer Blondes.
Anita Loos, title of book and film.

Play it, Sam. Play 'As Time Goes By'.
Ingrid Bergman, in 'Casablanca'.

Mean, Moody, Magnificent.
Anonymous caption
for poster of Jane Russell in 'The Outlaw', released 1946.

It took more than one man to change my name to Shanghai Lily.
Marlene Dietrich,
in 'Shanghai Express'.

You better come up and see me.
Mae West,
to Cary Grant in 'I'm No Angel'.

Beulah, peel me a grape.
Mae West, in 'I'm No Angel'.

In Italy for 30 years under the Borgias they had warfare, terror, murder, bloodshed. They produced Michaelangelo, Leonardo da Vinci and the Renaissance. In Switzerland they had brotherly love, 500 years of democracy and peace, and what did they produce? The cuckoo clock . . .
Orson Welles, in 'The Third Man'.

Of all the gin joints in all the towns in all the world, she walks into mine.
Humphrey Bogart, in 'Casablanca'.

Excuse me while I slip into something more comfortable.
Jean Harlow, in 'Hell's Angels'.

Here's looking at you kid.
Humphrey Bogart, in 'Casablanca'.

Live fast, die young and have a good-looking corpse.
John Derek, in 'Knock On Any Door'.

Mother of Mercy, is this the end of Rico?
Edward G. Robinson,
in 'Little Caesar'.

There are eight million stories in the naked city. This has been one of them.
Albert Maltz and Marvin Wald,
from 'The Naked City'.

A man's gotta do what a man's gotta do.
Alan Ladd, in 'Shane'.

Am I making myself clear, boys?
Mae West,
in 'She Done Him Wrong'.

If you want anything, just whistle.
Lauren Bacall,
in 'To Have and To Have Not.'

Yes, they have no bananas.
Thomas Mitchell,
as the Kid in 'Only Angels Have Wings'.

Rosebud!
Orson Welles, in 'Citizen Kane'.

What's up, Doc?
Bugs Bunny.

CENTRE: HUMPHREY BOGART AND INGRID BERGMAN IN 'CASABLANCA'.

LEFT: ALAN LADD IN 'SHANE'.

Index

A

B

C

D

E

F

G

H

I

J

K

L

M

N

O

P

Q

R

S

T

V

W

Y

Z